ADVANCE PRAISE FOR **WORKING ON THE WORK**

"Authentic student engagement in meaningful classroom work is the key to accountability. If teachers work on the work, accountability will take care of itself. Thanks, Phil Schlechty, for illuminating the way for all concerned educators and parents."
—Lawrence W. Lezotte, educational consultant and commentator, and author, *Learning for All* and *The Effective Schools Process*

"Schlechty takes everything he knows about education, places it in a user-friendly format, and delivers it to the schoolhouse. This book is such a valuable tool that I plan to discuss it, line by line, with my teachers."
—Judy Love, principal, Hayden Elementary School, Hayden, Indiana

"Any teacher who is interested in providing an authentically engaging classroom should embrace and utilize Phil Schlechty's WOW philosophy. It is an invaluable guide for teachers to become leaders and designers of quality lessons that facilitate student engagement and success."
—Kristin Barton, teacher, Gardenhill Elementary, La Mirada, California

"Once again Dr. Schlechty provides a must-read to the professional educator who is serious about improving and sustaining public education in our country."
—Ann Denlinger, superintendent, Durham Public Schools, Chapel Hill, North Carolina

Working on the Work

AN ACTION PLAN FOR TEACHERS, PRINCIPALS, AND SUPERINTENDENTS

Phillip C. Schlechty

JOSSEY-BASS
A Wiley Company
www.josseybass.com

Published by

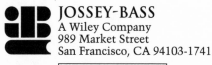

JOSSEY-BASS
A Wiley Company
989 Market Street
San Francisco, CA 94103-1741

www.josseybass.com

Copyright © 2002 by John Wiley & Sons, Inc.

Jossey-Bass is a registered trademark of John Wiley & Sons, Inc.

Jossey-Bass books and products are available through most bookstores. To contact Jossey-Bass directly, call (888) 378-2537, fax to (800) 605-2665, or visit our website at www.josseybass.com.

Substantial discounts on bulk quantities of Jossey-Bass books are available to corporations, professional associations, and other organizations. For details and discount information, contact the special sales department at Jossey-Bass.

We at Jossey-Bass strive to use the most environmentally sensitive paper stocks available to us. Our publications are printed on acid-free recycled stock whenever possible, and our paper always meets or exceeds minimum GPO and EPA requirements.

Library of Congress Cataloging-in-Publication Data

Schlechty, Phillip C., 1937-
  Working on the work : an action plan for teachers, principals, and superintendents / Phillip C. Schlechty.
    p.   cm. — (The Jossey-Bass education series)
Includes bibliographical references (p.   ) and index.
  ISBN 0-7879-6165-5 (alk. paper)
  1. School improvement programs—United States.   2. Academic achievement—United States.
3. Curriculum change—United States.   4. School environment—United States.   I. Title.   II. Series.
  LB2822.82 .S344 2002
  371.2—dc21   2002001833

FIRST EDITION

HB Printing   10 9

The Jossey-Bass Education Series

CONTENTS

Phillip C. Schlechty is founder and CEO of the Center for Leadership in School Reform and the author of *Reform in Teacher Education: A Sociological View* (1989), *Schools for the Twenty-First Century: Leadership Imperatives for Educational Reform* (1991), *Inventing Better Schools: An Action Plan for Educational Reform* (1997), and *Shaking Up the Schoolhouse: How to Support and Sustain Educational Innovation* (2000), as well as numerous other publications. Formerly a professor at the University of North Carolina at Chapel Hill and executive director of the Jefferson County Public Schools/Gheens Professional Development Academy, an organization he conceived and instituted, he serves as adviser to many school districts in the United States and Canada and conducts seminars and training sessions for superintendents, school board members, union leaders, principals, teachers, and parent groups.

Schlechty is one of the nation's most sought-after speakers on topics related to school reform. Business groups as well as educators find his perspective useful and understandable.

He received his B.S., M.A., and Ph.D. degrees from the Ohio State University.

Born near Rossburg, Ohio, Schlechty has two daughters, and he and his wife reside in Louisville, Kentucky.

The WOW School

Standard 1: Patterns of Engagement. Nearly all classes are highly engaged, and when they are not, teachers make every possible effort to redesign the pattern of activity in the classroom so that more students are authentically engaged.

Standard 2: Student Achievement. Parents, teachers, the principal, and the board of education, as well as others who have a stake in the performance of the schools, are satisfied with the level and type of learning that are occurring.

Standard 3: Content and Substance. Teachers and administrators have a clear, consistent, and shared understanding of what students are expected to know and to be able to do at various grade levels. This understanding is consistent with such official statements of expectations as state standards and standards established by local boards. Teachers and administrators also have a reasonable assessment of student interest in the topics suggested by these expectations and standards.

Standard 4: Organization of Knowledge. Teachers and support personnel (for example, media specialists) generally endeavor to ensure that the media, material, books, and visuals used to present information, propositions, ideas, and concepts to students are organized in ways that are most likely to appeal to the personal interests and aesthetic sensibilities of the largest possible number of students and to ensure as well that students have the skills needed to use these materials.

Standard 5: Product Focus. The tasks students are assigned and the activities they are encouraged to undertake are clearly linked in the minds of the teacher *and* the students to performances, products, and exhibitions about which the students care and on which students place value.

Standard 6: Clear and Compelling Product. When projects, performances, or exhibitions are part of the instructional design, students understand the standards by which these projects, performances, or exhibitions will be evaluated. They are committed to these standards and see the real prospect of meeting the stated standards if they work diligently at the tasks assigned and are encouraged.

Standard 7: A Safe Environment. Students and parents feel that the school as well as each classroom is a physically and psychologically safe place: success is expected and failure is understood as a necessary part of learning, there is mutual respect between and among faculty and students, and the fear of harm or harassment from fellow students and demeaning comments from teachers is negligible.

Standard 8: Affirmation of Performances. Persons who are significant in the lives of the student, including parents, siblings, peers, public audiences, and younger students, are positioned to observe, participate in, and benefit from student performances, as well as the products of those performances, and to affirm the significance and importance of the activity to be undertaken.

Standard 9: Affiliation. Students are provided opportunities to work with others (peers, parents, other adults, teachers, students from other schools or classrooms) on products, group performances, and exhibitions that they and others judge to be of significance.

Standard 10: Novelty and Variety. The range of tasks, products, and exhibitions is wide and varied, and the technologies that students are encouraged to employ are varied as well, moving from the simplest and well understood (for example, a pen and a piece of paper) to the most complex (for example, sophisticated computer applications).

Standard 11: Choice. What students are to learn is usually not subject to negotiation, but they have considerable choice and numerous options in what they will do and how they will go about doing those things in order to learn.

Standard 12: Authenticity. The tasks students are assigned and the work they are encouraged to undertake have meaning and significance in their lives now and are related to consequences to which they attach importance.

Introduction

Schools cannot be made great by great teacher performances. They will only be made great by great student performance.

Nowadays, public school educators are under increasing pressure to improve student academic performance. There are at least three ways educators might respond to this pressure. They can:

- Work on the students.
- Work on the teachers.
- Work on the work.

Teachers who have tried the first approach have had little success; cajoling students or even threatening them sometimes produces compliance, but it does not produce the commitment needed to perform at high levels. Bribing students and pandering to their whims sometimes generates temporary enthusiasm, but it is hard to sustain enthusiasm based on frivolous goals. In the long run, working on the students just does not work.

School administrators who have tried the second strategy have had no more success than have the teachers who have tried the first strategy. Some school district leaders have tried bribing teachers with merit pay, only to discover that teachers are already doing all they know how to do. Some administrators have tried observation schemes that rival the best time and motion studies in factory settings, only to find that teaching cannot be rationalized in this manner. These efforts have consumed much energy and stirred considerable debate, but the results have not been impressive.

My intent in writing this book is to advance a third alternative. It is written for school superintendents and principals who are prepared to abandon the idea that they can somehow improve student learning by working on teachers and who are prepared to embrace the notion that their job is to work *with* teachers to improve the quality of the work teachers provide to students. This book is written for teachers who are prepared to give up on working on students and to begin to concentrate their attention on working on the work they provide to students.

THE BASIC THEME

After speaking on the subject for nearly a decade, I wrote *Schools for the Twenty-First Century: Leadership Imperatives for Educational Reform* (Schlechty, 1990), in which I advanced the idea that the key to school success is to be found in identifying or creating engaging schoolwork for students. So many teachers and principals became excited by these ideas that I was encouraged to develop them further. By 1992, the ideas had been clarified to the point that some who were using these concepts in training programs began to refer to the "WOW framework," or to use the label (some might say slogan), "Working on the Work." As the ideas underlying this framework became clearer, I wrote two more books: *Inventing Better Schools: An Action Plan for Educational Reform* (1997) and *Shaking Up the Schoolhouse: How to Support and Sustain Educational Innovation* (2000). Both address a wide range of issues that need to be considered by educators concerned with improving America's schools, in addition to issues associated with the WOW framework. This book, unlike its predecessors, centers on only one issue: the uses of the WOW framework as a tool to improve student performance in school.

The key to school success is to be found in identifying or creating engaging schoolwork for students.

SCHOOLWORK: A COMMONPLACE TERM

In their everyday lives, teachers understand that what they are about is designing work for their students and trying to get students engaged in the work. Words like *schoolwork, homework,* and *student work* fall easily from the lips of most teachers and school administrators.

Unfortunately, when it comes to discussing pedagogy, teachers and those who work with them spend much more time trying to understand learning styles and teaching styles than they spend trying to understand the nature of the work teachers assign to students or the work teachers encourage students to undertake. My intent here is to make schoolwork the centerpiece as a source of explanation of variance in student performance and student learning.

ON THE NATURE OF SCHOOLWORK

Work is goal-oriented activity and therefore is purposeful activity. Unlike play, it is intended to produce something of use, regardless of whether the "worker" is producing something only for himself or herself or whether the product is for the use of others. The artist who is producing a painting for personal enjoyment is engaged in a form of work, just as are the poet, the actor, and the person who works on an assembly line.

There are two kinds of work: manual work and knowledge work. Manual work involves the application of muscle, sinew, and brawn to complete tasks, produce products, and achieve goals. Knowledge work involves the applications of intellectual processes (for example, problem-solving skills); the management and control of symbols, propositions, and other forms of knowledge; and the use of these intellectual products in the achievement of goals.

Both forms of work are purposeful activity aimed toward some result or outcome that is assumed to be of value to one's self and others. They differ in that one type of work involves primarily the use of the body with only limited intellectual demands; the other has high-intellectual demands and only limited physical requirements.[1]

Schoolwork, at least as the term is used here, refers to those tasks, activities, and experiences that teachers design for students and those that teachers encourage students to design for themselves, which the teacher assumes will result in students' learning what it is intended that they should learn. Schoolwork is a special form of knowledge work: a form intended to produce learning assumed to be essential to the continuation of the culture and the optimization of the moral and intellectual development of the individual student.

Schoolwork is a form of work intended to produce learning.

Working on the Work entails teachers' purposefully creating, designing, identifying, or otherwise making available to students authentically engaging activities, programs, tasks, assignments, and opportunities to practice that result in students' learning those things it is determined that students need to learn to be judged well educated. Working on the Work is purposeful activity by teachers that results in purposeful activity by students.

THE RESEARCH BASE

For those who insist that the only way to improve schools is to proceed on the basis of "the research," this book will be a disappointment. No systematic research program has been directed at assessing the impact of the WOW approach on improving schools. The primary reason this is so is that WOW is not a program. It is a system of thought and a way of life.

WOW is not intended to replace or even to compete with existing efforts to improve instruction. It certainly is not intended to serve as a substitute for competent teachers in the classroom. Rather, it is a framework for giving direction and purpose to much that is already going on in schools and classrooms and a framework that leads to suggestions regarding what might need to be going on. As Paul Hagerty, a superintendent with experience with the WOW framework, has observed, "It is not a program; it is an operating system." Furthermore, it is an operating system with which many research-based programs are compatible.

Readers who continue to be concerned about this matter may find some comfort in the fact that the WOW framework encourages nothing that violates current research findings. Indeed, much that is contained in the framework was suggested to me by the research on teaching and learning. It accommodates any improvement effort that is focused on ensuring that students are authentically engaged in the tasks they are provided and on ensuring, as well, that these tasks cause students to work on and with knowledge that the adult community has judged to be important for students to learn.

Many of the ideas suggested by the WOW framework do, however, go beyond the research. This is as it should be. As Rosabeth Moss Kanter (1997) observes, "Sometimes an idea stems from significant scientific and technical research, but just as often the need for R&D follows the idea (as in the development of technology that made colored paint stick to metal car bodies). What is always essential, however, is the idea itself: a concept resulting from new thinking" (p. 8).

BASIC ASSUMPTIONS

The WOW framework requires new thinking. This thinking is perhaps best summarized in terms of the assumptions on which the framework is based:

1. One of the primary tasks of teachers is to provide work for students: work that students engage in and from which students learn that which it is intended that they learn.

2. A second task of teachers is to lead students to do well and successfully the work they undertake.

3. Therefore, teachers are leaders and inventors, and students are volunteers.

4. What students have to volunteer is their attention and commitment.

5. Differences in commitment and attention produce differences in student engagement.

6. Differences in the level and type of engagement affect directly the effort that students expend on school-related tasks.

7. Effort affects learning outcomes at least as much as does intellectual ability.

8. The level and type of engagement will vary depending on the qualities teachers build into the work they provide students.

9. Therefore, teachers can directly affect student learning through the invention of work that has those qualities that are most engaging to students.

If these assumptions are firmly embraced and acted on, I am persuaded that there would be a dramatic increase in the effectiveness of our schools. Unfortunately, these assumptions are seldom reflected in textbooks on teaching.

> ### Basic Assumptions
>
> 1. One of the primary tasks of teachers is to provide work for students: work that students engage in and from which students learn that which it is intended that they learn.
> 2. A second task of teachers is to lead students to do well and successfully the work they undertake.
> 3. Therefore, teachers are leaders and inventors, and students are volunteers.
> 4. What students have to volunteer is their attention and commitment.
> 5. Differences in commitment and attention produce differences in student engagement.
> 6. Differences in the level and type of engagement affect directly the effort that students expend on school-related tasks.
> 7. Effort affects learning outcomes at least as much as does intellectual ability.
> 8. The level and type of engagement will vary depending on the qualities teachers build into the work they provide students.
> 9. Therefore, teachers can directly affect student learning through the invention of work that has those qualities that are most engaging to students.

THE ROLE OF THE TEACHER

Great teachers are great leaders. As leaders, great teachers understand that the needs and interests of those they want to follow them, the students, must be central to their concerns. They understand this because they know that good leaders are also good followers. (See Kelly, 1988, and Schlechty, 1990.)

Great teachers are great leaders.

The idea that teachers are, or should be, leaders is not new. As long ago as 1932, Willard Waller dedicated a large section of his now-classic book, *The Sociology of Teaching,* to a discussion of the teacher as an institutional leader as well as what he called a "personal leader" (see Waller, [1932] 1967).

Teachers do lead, but most teachers do not view themselves as leaders. As Waller observes about such persons, "They lead spontaneously, and perhaps without any awareness of the fact that they are leading" (Waller, [1932] 1967, p. 189). Rather than seeing themselves as leaders, most teachers see themselves as performers, clinicians, diagnosticians, and conveyers of information. When they do see themselves in some sort of authoritative role, they are more likely to see themselves as managers and controllers than as leaders and directors.

FACILITATOR, COACH, OR LEADER?

The phrase *facilitator of learning* has gained some popularity in recent years. Properly understood, facilitation is a leadership role. Unfortunately, some who use the word *facilitation* to describe teaching seem to see the teacher more as a midwife than a leader.

Those who argue that the primary task of the teacher is to facilitate learning are also prone to use words and phrases like *personal development* and *the personal construction of knowledge* when they describe the ends of education. I have no problem with this argument, so long as it also acknowledges that transmitting the collective wisdom of the group is also important. Schools, especially in democracies, serve social ends and have social consequences, as well as serving personal ends and producing personal consequences. Duty and obligation are as much a part of the equation as are rights and needs. As leaders, teachers are not only responsible for responding to the needs of those they lead; teachers must also ensure that those they lead respond to ends that may not be immediately appealing to students, though essential to the functioning of a democratic society.

For those who find this view offensive, especially the more ideological among those who call themselves constructivists, it would be well to remember that even John Dewey, to whom many constructivist refer for support, was not opposed to the teaching of traditional subjects. Indeed, Dewey's laboratory school gave traditional subjects a central place in the curriculum. What he opposed was the way these subjects were taught. He was not opposed to memorization. He was opposed to meaningless rote learning. As Diane Ravitch (2000) has observed, however, "Many of Dewey's disciples drew the wrong lessons from the Dewey school. They seemed to think that the liberation of children from formal instruction was an end in itself. Dewey did not agree" (p. 172).

Great teachers know that students have a limited and truncated view of the world around them and perhaps a distorted view of their own potential and capabilities.[2] As leaders, teachers are obligated to help students move in directions students might initially want to avoid and, as well, to cause students to test themselves in circumstances in which they feel uncomfortable and uncertain. Great leaders have empathetic understanding with regard to these matters, but they do not let this understanding preclude them from insisting on more than students sometimes initially believe they can do. It is in this sense that Theodore Sizer's notion (1984) of the teacher as coach has more appeal than does the idea of teacher as facilitator; at least this is so for me. But because I also believe that teachers must do more than either coaches or facilitators do, I prefer to use the more generic term *leader* when I discuss the role of teacher.[3]

LEADERS MUST LEAD

The primary function of a leader is to inspire others to do things they might otherwise not do and encourage others to go in directions they might not otherwise pursue. Certainly, great leaders must respond to the needs, interests, and concerns of those they hope will follow them, but make no mistake about it, *one of the obligations of the leader is to lead.*

The primary function of a leader is to inspire others to do things they might otherwise not do.

Sometimes this leadership involves nothing more (or less) than helping members of the group being led to figure out where they want to go and then helping them get there. Sometimes it is helping those being led to see directions they might go that they would not otherwise have thought of and then inspiring them to go in those directions. Sometimes leaders must try to get others to do things they are reluctant to do, even when it would be easier to allow others to do what they want to do or are comfortable doing. Great leaders are those who are best at figuring out when to push and when to comply.

Viewing the teacher as a leader does cause some problems for those who advance what I have come to refer to as context-oblivious solutions to educational problems. For example, there are some in education who hold that it is possible to define best teaching practice with little or no attention to the situation in which the teaching occurs. Indeed, some are so oblivious to the significance of context that they do not even discuss the matter; they simply assume that context is largely irrelevant. What is important are the characteristics of the teacher and what the teacher does.[4]

Like other leaders, great teachers understand that best practice cannot be defined outside the context in which it occurs. What is best practice in one context may be malpractice in the next. They know that the time of day, the experiences students have had in working together, the culture of the school, and the way other teachers operate all affect what they can do and must do, and they understand as well that this context is ever changing.

Those who are most prone to being context oblivious also tend to view teachers as clinicians and diagnosticians. Their quest quite often is for a context-oblivious set of behaviors that the teacher can manifest that will produce the intended learning results. What nonsense!

Leaders do diagnose, but they do so in order to get others to do things. It is not the goal of the leader to do things to others. Teachers are not physical therapists or surgeons or members of any other occupational group that engages in clinical practice.

Teachers are a special subset of a larger category called *leaders* that include clergy, business executives, and military officers. What teachers have in common with these other leaders is that they, like these other leaders, are trying to get others to do things they might not otherwise do: to pursue goals they might not otherwise pursue and to accomplish things they might not otherwise accomplish.

But teachers are not clerics or executives or military officers. They are, after all, teachers, and the special task of teachers is to engage students in activities, tasks, assignments, and other undertakings that result in students' learning things they need to learn but might not learn unless they are properly led. Because teachers are leaders, they can learn from other leaders, but because they are teachers, they are also unique, just as other types of leaders are unique.

COMPETENCE AND COMMITMENT

When it comes to ensuring student success, there is nothing more important than a competent and committed teacher. The questions are, At what should the teacher

- The teacher needs to be skilled in providing students with schoolwork that will engage them and encourage them to direct their efforts in productive ways.
- The teacher needs to be committed to ensuring that the work he or she provides students results in their working with the knowledge they are expected to acquire in order to be entitled to be called well educated. The teacher also needs to be committed to providing students with instruction and practice in the skills that will be of continuing value to them as they mature.

be competent? and To what should the teacher be committed? The WOW approach answers these questions as follows:

- The teacher needs to be skilled in providing students with schoolwork that will engage them and encourage them to direct their efforts in productive ways.

- The teacher needs to be committed to ensuring that the work he or she provides students results in their working with the knowledge they are expected to acquire in order to be entitled to be called well educated. The teacher also needs to be committed to providing students with instruction and practice in the skills that will be of continuing value to them as they mature.

To do these things, teachers need a disciplined approach to creating engaging work for students. They also need a framework for determining whether what they are trying to teach their students is what they should be expecting students to learn. The WOW framework provides such an approach.

THE IMPORTANCE OF DISCIPLINE

When educators speak of discipline, it is usually in reference to students—for example, that one of them is a "discipline problem." There is, however, another meaning for the word. As used here, the word *discipline* has to do with the idea of regimen or a regularized manner of approaching a problem or task. Disciplines have a point of view (the chemist looks at the world from a different point of view than does the physicist). Working on the Work provides a disciplined view of the art and science of teaching.

The function of disciplines is to ensure control and coherence. To say that one is disciplined in the sense the word is used here is to say that one proceeds from a coherent point of view that suggests where one might look for answers when things get "out of control" or when things do not happen the way it is assumed they should happen.

WOW is what Kanter (1997) refers to as a "process discipline." She writes:

> Process disciplines establish control that does not constrain. Total quality management (TQM) programs, for example, provide a common set of analytic and problem-solving techniques to be used in every part of the organization, regardless of the subdisciplines involved in particular functions like engineering or marketing. The "inspiration" part of quality programs (leaders encouraging quality values) is often less important than the "perspiration" component (people using analytic tools to manage difficult trade-offs on their own). Process disciplines such as planning routines or problem-solving techniques guide action without constraining the form that action takes. And it is easier for people to work together when they share such disciplines [pp. 159–160].

Discipline is not antithetical to creativity and innovation; indeed, it makes creativity possible. Without shared disciplines, the only form of control is arbitrary authority. It is arbitrary authority rather than shared disciplines that stifle creativity. As Kanter (1997) observes, "Empowerment cannot mean setting everyone loose to do whatever they want, however they want to do it" (p. 159). She notes, "Disciplines are not necessarily antithetical to creativity, however. They can be the grounding that permits creativity. After all, intuition often stems from deep knowledge gained through constant practice, which then permits imaginative leaps" (p. 162). Used consistently and collectively, the WOW framework can provide school faculties with such an empowering discipline—or so I believe.

ENGAGING WORK AND ENGAGING TEACHERS

The words *engaged, engagement,* and *engaging* contain complex and subtle meanings. One set of meanings has to do with obligations, duties, and commitments, as in, "She is engaged to be married" or "Her fiancé engaged the services of a minister." Another set has to do with involvement, as "to draw into, entangle, attract, or hold." And another set, especially attached to the word *engaging,* has to do with pleasantness, winning ways, and charm.[5]

The confusion that can result from these multiple meanings is nowhere so clear as when one uses the words *engagement* and *engaging* in the context of pedagogical discussions. When one says, for example, that a teacher is engaging, does this mean that the teacher possesses personal qualities that are attractive to students— that is, that the teacher is pleasant, winning, charming, or perhaps even "charismatic"? Or does it mean that the teacher creates activities for students that draw them in, attract them, hold them, and fasten their attention? Sometimes it seems to mean one of these things, sometimes the other, and sometimes both.

It is an unfortunate fact that educators too often fail to differentiate between teachers who are engaging as a person or as a performer and teachers who are skilled at providing work and activities for students that the students find to be engaging. Failure to make this distinction too often leads to the conclusion that the only way to improve education is to work on the performance of the teachers. This eventually leads to the hopeless conclusion that the only way to improve the schools is to make it possible to recruit to the schools 2.7 million college-educated Americans who are personally engaging and willing to provide heroic personal performances on a routine basis for a relatively modest financial reward.

There are, of course, some teachers who, by force of personality, charm, and wit, are able to inspire students to perform even when the subject is difficult or inherently uninteresting. Heroic teachers do exist, but they cannot be the stuff of which great schools are made. There is simply not enough heroic material to go around. What is needed are teachers who know how to create, as a matter of routine practice, schoolwork that engages students. Schools cannot be made great by great teacher performances. They will only be made great by great student performance.[6]

A more hopeful view would be to accept that people who have the personal qualities needed to hold any audience spellbound for any length of time are in short supply, and persons who by dint of personality can cause others to do things they might not otherwise do are in short supply as well. What is in virtually unlimited supply, once teachers figure out how to do it, are tasks, assignments, and activities that students find engaging from which the students learn those things that teachers and the larger society believe the students should learn.[7]

ORGANIZATION OF THE BOOK

This book is written on the assumption that most readers have already read *Shaking Up the Schoolhouse,* and some have read *Schools for the Twenty-First Century* and *Inventing Better Schools.* Therefore, I will not try here, as I do in those books, to persuade readers that the perspective being advanced is a worthy one. I simply assume that readers are already convinced that this is so and are interested in figuring out how to act on what they now believe to be the case.

Given this assumption, in Chapter One, I discuss the idea of engagement and suggest some strategies for assessing engagement and encouraging school faculties to make engagement a central concern in their discussions.

In Chapter Two, I present twelve descriptors of schools that, taken together, constitute a vision of what a school where the WOW framework is in place would look like (these descriptors appear at the beginning of this Introduction). These descriptors derive in large part from the WOW framework presented in earlier publications, especially *Shaking Up the Schoolhouse,* but here I elaborate on and refine them beyond what was presented there. I also provide a set of questions that might be used to create dialogue within a faculty, as well as a guide for personal reflection and self-examination. These questions have been framed so that they correspond to twelve descriptors of a WOW school.

Chapter Three is directed primarily to teachers, but principals and superintendents should read it as well. A teacher operating independently can probably do some things to improve what goes on in her or his classroom by systematically applying the WOW framework to what she or he is about. However, for this framework to have optimal effect, it requires a school culture where collegial conversations about teaching are the norm and where the principal sees his or her role as one that requires working with teachers and working on the work rather than working on the teachers themselves.

Chapter Four is written for principals who sincerely want to lead an effort to transform the school they lead into a school where the ideas on which WOW is based are deeply embedded in the culture of the school. Without such principals, the long-term and systematic impact of the WOW framework will never be realized.

Not all teachers work in schools where the principal is knowledgeable about or committed to the ideas being advanced here. For such teachers, it is important to understand what their principal might be able to do for them so that they are in a better position to lead those who are, by virtue of the position they occupy, charged with the responsibility of leading them. Sometimes followers must lead their leaders. Thus many teachers will benefit from reading this chapter, even though it is written with principals in mind.

It is one of the ironies of the school reform literature that so little has been written about the relationship between superintendents and principals. It is as though superintendents and principals are assumed to operate in separate universes, bumping into each other only on occasion, and most typically those occasions are shaped more by the needs of central office staff than by the needs of the principals themselves.

The superintendent who is to lead the kind of reform suggested in this book needs to have a clear image of what a school would look like if it were organized to work on the work. The superintendent also needs to have a clear understanding of what he or she should expect principals to do and the kind of support principals and teachers need to do these things. Thus the superintendent should read Chapters Three and Four, even though they are directed primarily to teachers and principals.

Chapter Five, which is written for superintendents, provides concrete suggestions and advice for what superintendents who are committed to making the WOW framework the basis for the "way we do business around here." Some of the observations also derive from my understanding of the literature related to leading change in America's corporate structure and the role of the chief executive officer (CEO) in leading those changes. (Those who have read my previous work know that I view the superintendent as a CEO and believe that schools are better served when superintendents view themselves in this way as well.) Teachers and principals can also benefit from reading Chapter Five, if for no other reason than that it will help them develop further the systemwide perspective they need to develop if the changes they are trying to advance are to be more than a passing fad sponsored by one or two inspired principals and a small cadre of dedicated teachers.

The appendixes of this book are a vital part of it. For the most part, they are based on the framework presented in Chapter Two and are organized to facilitate the kinds of discussion, analysis, and action planning suggested throughout this book.

Appendix A has at least three uses:

• A principal acting alone might use the descriptors provided as a guide in developing a personal and private assessment of the extent to which the operating style of the school he or she leads is consistent with the WOW framework. Used in this way, a principal might treat the framework as a questionnaire and respond to it based on his or her own immediate impressions (as a guide to personal reflection). Or he or she might take on an extended investigation intended to produce data to give more confidence that the answers provided are consistent with the facts of the case.

• A superintendent might use these descriptors as a means of introducing principals to a vision of a school organized around the WOW framework (see Chapter Five).

• A principal might have teachers assess the school in terms of the descriptors provided and then use the results of these assessments as a basis for faculty dialogue (see Chapter Four).

The descriptors presented in Appendix B are designed for classroom teachers. Teachers can use them as a guide for personal reflection and also as a framework or lens through which they can analyze or evaluate proposed units of study to determine whether the design includes the qualities of work needed to increase the likelihood of authentic engagement. The same framework can be used as a guide to a critical review of past activity that has not produced the intended levels of engagement.

It is my hope that this book will be helpful to those teachers and other educational leaders who believe, as I do, that the public schools of America can be reinvented in ways that come to grips with the emerging realities of the twenty-first century. If this is to happen, however, teachers and other school leaders must be much more intentional that they have ever been before about pursuing what I take to be the core business of schools: the business of inventing schoolwork for students that truly engages their hearts and minds and results in all students' learning what they need to learn to be entitled to be called well educated.

ACKNOWLEDGMENTS

In writing this book I have had the opportunity to have literally hundreds of teachers and principals review early drafts. Many of these persons have provided useful comments. I would like to thank each of them personally, but there are too many to list here. I hope this acknowledgment makes each of these persons aware that I know that I am in their debt.

As always, the staff at the Center for Leadership in School Reform (CLSR) has been supportive of my efforts, and I want to thank each of them for their help. In the case of this book, however, several persons should be recognized individually.

First, Tena Lutz, who has worked with me on every book I have written since 1984, has continued her great work. Without her support, I would write much less, and I suspect less well. Thanks, Tena.

Hugh Cassell who, like Tena, has been with me through every book I have written since 1984 has once again given me invaluable editorial advice. Thanks once again, Hugh.

This book would not have been written had it not been for Marilyn Hohmann, now a colleague at the Center for Leadership in School Reform and formerly one of America's great high school principals. She has insisted for many years that a user-friendly handbook was needed if Working on the Work was to become embedded deeply in the culture of schools. This handbook is my response to her persistent request.

I also want to acknowledge a huge debt I owe to Ronald Barber, a longtime friend and colleague. Ron passed away this year, but for sixteen years, he and I worked together on many projects that helped me to develop the ideas that are presented here. I first met Ron when he was the principal of a middle school, and I was trying to create a leadership development system (the Gheens Academy) for the Jefferson County (Kentucky) Public Schools. When I later created the Center for Leadership in School Reform, Ron Barber and Marilyn Hohmann, along with Tena Lutz, became key individuals in the organization I was trying to build.

All of us at CLSR miss Ron. He was a great leader and a great friend; his passing leaves a hole in my life. I learned much from him and continue to reflect on what I learned. Once again, I want to acknowledge the contribution that Ron has made to the development of the Working on the Work framework.

The editorial and production staff at Jossey-Bass Publishers has worked hard to make the final stages of producing a book as painless (for the author) as possible. It is still painful, but it is better than it used to be. Thanks to all of you, and I would especially like to thank Lesley Iura who has stuck with me through some trying times.

Finally, no list of acknowledgments would be complete without saying thank-you to my wife, Shelia. Without her, I would not be a position to write this book, to say nothing of the books I have written in the past. She no longer types my manuscripts, but she continues to provide the encouragement I need to keep at the task.

Notes

1. Digging a ditch does involve some level of intellectual activity, just as writing requires a certain amount of hand-eye coordination, but the fact that intellectual work is different in kind from manual work seems clear enough to leave the matter here.

2. Students are, after all, children with only limited experiences. They are uneducated. That is why they are in school. Sometimes an overly romanticized view of children leads to the conclusion that all that children need to know, they already possess. Rousseau may have believed this. I do not. Part of the task of schooling is to introduce students to the culture in which they will function and provide them with the tools they will need to negotiate that culture in ways that benefit themselves and others. Learning how to learn is hard work, and sometimes it is not enjoyable work. As leaders and as responsible adults, teachers are obliged to encourage students to do what they need to do, as well as to support them in doing what they want to do.

3. Theodore Sizer has had a profound impact on the way I think about some educational issues. I really have no problem with his metaphor of the teacher as coach. The way he uses this term is quite consistent with the meaning I attach to the word *leader*. For reasons that I make clear elsewhere, however, I am less comfortable with his notion of the student as worker (see Schlechty, 1991, 1997, 2000).

4. I made a conscious decision not to provide specific references here. I do not want to start a quarrel with any one person. I know there are many who write about best practice who are very sensitive to issues of context. I do not want to spend the time here distinguishing among those who are context sensitive and those who are not. I assume readers are intelligent and can discover for themselves that there are many who write about best practice who do not give context enough attention. This group seems to believe that what works in the fall works equally well in the spring; what works to enhance the development of low-level skills works equally well to encourage high-level thought; what works to raise test scores also works to improve learning; and what works to condition pigeons and rats works equally well to prepare citizens for a democracy.

5. See *Webster's New World Dictionary of the American Language.*

6. The personal qualities, skills, and attributes of teachers do make a difference, and I do not dismiss this fact. It is my belief, however, that significant improvement in student learning is more likely to be forthcoming if all teachers can be

brought to be at least as concerned with the quality of the tasks they provide for students as they are about the quality of their own performance.

7. Although I have no research to support my view (I also know of none that challenges it), I have some doubts about the overall efficacy of teacher personality and teacher performance as being a powerful determinant of student learning in general. I have no doubt that there are some—perhaps even many—students who learn more from an engaging teacher than from a teacher who is less engaging. However, even the most engaging teacher will not be engaging to all students and perhaps not even to most students. Furthermore, even those who find the teacher most engaging are likely to become disenchanted from time to time. Certainly, most of us have warm memories of a teacher we found to be engaging. If we examine those memories carefully, however, it often turns out that what made the teacher engaging was not what the teacher did, but what the teacher encouraged us to do and the care he or she took to ensure that what we were asked to do had meaning and significance in our own lives.

Working on the Work

Making Engagement Central

*If students become engaged in the right "stuff," they are likely to learn
what we want them to learn.*

In *Shaking Up the Schoolhouse* (Schlechty, 2000), I distinguish among
five types of responses students might make to any school task (see
Figure 1.1):

- *Authentic engagement.* The task, activity, or work the student is assigned or encouraged to undertake is associated with a result or outcome that has clear
  meaning and relatively immediate value to the student—for example, reading
  a book on a topic of personal interest to the student or to get access to information that the student needs to solve a problem of real interest to him or her.

- *Ritual engagement.* The immediate end of the assigned work has little or no in-
  herent meaning or direct value to the student, but the student associates it with
  extrinsic outcomes and results that are of value—for example, reading a book
  in order to pass a test or to earn grades needed to be accepted at college.[1]

- *Passive compliance.* The student is willing to expend whatever effort is needed
  to avoid negative consequences, although he or she sees little meaning in the
  tasks assigned or the consequences of doing those tasks.

- *Retreatism.* The student is disengaged from the tasks, expends no energy in attempting to comply with the demands of the tasks, but does not act in ways that
  disrupt others and does not try to substitute other activities for the assigned task.

- *Rebellion.* The student summarily refuses to do the task assigned, acts in ways
  that disrupt others, or attempts to substitute tasks and activities to which he or

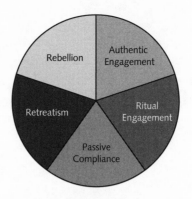

Figure 1.1.
Student Responses To Schoolwork.

she is committed in lieu of those assigned or supported by the school and by the teacher.

Given this typology, it becomes possible to characterize classrooms in terms of the patterns of engagement that are observed. These characterizations are based on the following assumptions:

- Any given student will be engaged in different ways in different tasks, and sometimes this engagement will differ with regard to the same task. For example, a student who normally finds a task authentically engaging may resort to retreatism on a given day or at a given moment simply because he or she is tired or distracted by other concerns. Sometimes the same student may be passively compliant, and at other times the only thing that is compelling about the task is what its accomplishment makes possible in another arena (perhaps eligibility to play football). The issue is not the presence or absence of these different forms of engagement but the pattern these forms create over time.

Any given student will be engaged in different ways in different tasks—at times, even with regard to the same task.

- Retreatism, passive compliance, and ritual engagement are not in themselves indicators of pathology in the classroom. Furthermore, a student who is ritually engaged or passively compliant or in a retreatist mode is not necessarily "misbehaving." In fact, it is not at all clear that anyone could tolerate—emotionally and physically—being engaged authentically all the time. Retreatism may be a resting point for a student who has otherwise been authentically engaged throughout the activity.

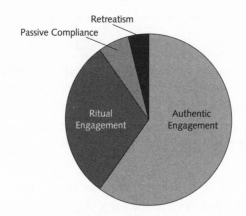

Figure 1.2.
Student Responses in the Highly Engaged Classroom.

• As schools are now organized, student success, especially success in doing well in an environment that places emphasis on high test scores, does not require authentic engagement.[2] In fact, many of the strategies that are being advanced to improve test scores are nothing more or less than efforts to increase passive compliance and ritual engagement and decrease retreatism and rebellion.[3]

• Each of the types of engagement represents a different type or category of response rather than a different point on a continuum. A student who is ritually engaged is engaged in a different way than is a student who is authentically engaged. Those who are ritually engaged are not necessarily less engaged than are those who are authentically engaged; they are engaged for a different reason or set of reasons. Similarly, passive compliance is a distinct type of engagement. Unlike either authentic engagement or ritual engagement, however, passive compliance is likely to be motivated more by avoidance of punishment or unpleasant consequences than by any type of positive goal or outcome.

• It is assumed that different types of engagement produce different types of commitment and, therefore, different types of effort and learning results. Here it is important to note that I proceed from the hunch—and at this point it is nothing more than a hunch—that students who are ritually engaged do learn what they need to learn to do well on tests and satisfy the demands of adult authority, although they probably retain less of what they have "learned" than would be the case if they were authentically engaged. Indeed, students who are

Figure 1.3.
Student Responses in the Well-Managed Classroom.

ritually engaged are likely to be so concerned with what is going to be on the test that they will be reluctant to undertake any task that does not have some clear payoff in terms of extrinsic values associated with such performance measures.[4]

THE HIGHLY ENGAGED CLASSROOM

In the highly engaged classroom, most students are authentically engaged most of the time (see Figure 1.2). There are also, however, considerable ritual engagement, some passive compliance, and maybe even a limited amount of retreatism. Rebellion may also occur in the highly engaged classroom, but it will be idiosyncratic and will not be sustained long enough to be patterned. In summary, most students in the highly engaged classroom are authentically engaged most of the time, and all students are authentically engaged some of the time. It is also a classroom that has little or no rebellion, limited retreatism, and limited passive compliance.

THE WELL-MANAGED CLASSROOM

The well-managed classroom has considerably less authentic engagement than does the highly engaged classroom (see Figure 1.3). It also has considerably more passive compliance and retreatism. Ritual engagement, as opposed to authentic engagement, is the dominant mode of response in the well-managed classroom. As in the highly engaged classroom, there is little or no rebellion.

Because such a classroom is orderly and most students seem to do the work assigned—some with a degree of enthusiasm—it is easy for the teacher and the outside observer to confuse the well-managed classroom with the highly engaged classroom. The well-managed classroom appears well managed not because students are authentically engaged but because they are willing to be compliant. As long as the teacher and the principal fail to ask the right questions of students, the absence of authentic engagement will probably go unnoticed, though the effects on learning may be quite real. (See, for example, Pope, 2001.)

THE PATHOLOGICAL CLASSROOM

The pathological classroom looks very much like the well-managed classroom except for the presence of patterned rebellion (see Figure 1.4). The rebellion is not limited to isolated cases. Many students actively reject the task assigned or substitute other activity to replace what has been officially assigned or expected. (Cheating is a form of rebellion too.)

Furthermore, it seems likely that in the effort to reduce rebellion, teachers in the pathological classroom often settle for retreatism or passive compliance and "work on the students" to gain such a response. Indeed, although I have no empirical evidence on which to base my hunch, I would bet that teachers in pathological classrooms tend to lower performance expectations to the point that passive compliance gets higher rewards (better grades) than would be produced in a highly engaged classroom. This could be one source of the grade inflation that is of such concern to some critics of public schools.

Nevertheless, there is likely to be some degree of authentic engagement even in the pathological classroom. For example, the subject being taught may be of such interest to a particular student that he or she finds meaning in the tasks even when the tasks are poorly designed.

There is likely to be considerable ritual engagement as well; some students need the grade to get into college, or they so fear displeasing their parents that they do whatever they need to do to get the teacher's approval. The incidence of passive compliance will also be high, as will be the incidence of retreatism. Indeed, it is the increase in retreatism and the presence of patterns of rebellion that distinguish the pathological classroom from the well-managed classroom.

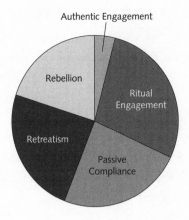

Figure 1.4.
Student Responses in the Pathological Classroom.

Classrooms and Engagement

Highly Engaged Classroom

A classroom in which most students are authentically engaged most of the time, all students are authentically engaged most of the time, and all students are authentically engaged some of the time. It is also a classroom that has little or no rebellion, limited retreatism, and limited passive compliance.

The Well-Managed Classroom

The well-managed classroom appears well managed, not because students are authentically engaged but because they are willing to be compliant. As long as the teacher and the principal fail to ask the right questions of the students, the absence of authentic engagement will likely not be noticed.

The Pathological Classroom

The pathological classroom looks very much like the well-managed classroom except for the presence of patterned rebellion. In the pathological classroom, many students actively reject the task assigned or the substitution of other activity to replace what has been officially assigned or expected (or both). (Cheating is a form of rebellion.)

DEVELOPING AN ENGAGEMENT PROFILE

One of the first steps in moving toward continuously improving the quality of the work provided to students is to center attention on the patterns of engagement in a classroom or set of classrooms.[5] An individual teacher operating alone can do much to understand better what is going on in his or her classroom. For example, using the rubrics provided later in this chapter as a guide, teachers can develop a profile of their own classroom, whether or not the principal or the colleagues join them. I have found, however, that leadership by a principal and support from colleagues increase the likelihood that teachers will stick with the process long enough to make it a routine part of their school lives.

Teachers can develop a profile of their own classroom to understand better what is going on.

There are a variety of ways to generate the energy needed to sustain a group effort. One that I have observed to work well includes beginning with an "all-hands" workshop where the faculty is made aware of the basic ideas underlying the WOW model.[6] Following the initial workshop, principals are encouraged to work with volunteer teachers to develop an engagement profile for the school.

At the same time, volunteer teachers are encouraged to develop profiles of their own classroom along the lines suggested by Figures 1.1 through 1.4. By making comparisons between two points in time (say, week 1 compared to week 2), teachers are able to see, in graphic terms, how patterns of engagement in their classroom vary from day to day and task to task. As teachers begin to see such variance, they begin to ask why this is so. Most teachers already understand, intuitively at least, that the nature of the work they assign to students has a considerable bearing on this matter. Initially, however, some teachers may seek explanations in such factors as the time of day, the day of the week, and maybe even the sign of the moon. Eventually, most teachers come to embrace the notion that the tasks that they assign to students are one of the few variables under their control that directly affect student engagement. It is at this point that the WOW framework begins to make real sense to teachers. When they come to believe that they can make a direct and immediate difference in something they care about (and they do care about student engagement), they have a reason to work on the work.

*Patterns of engagement vary
from day to day and task to task.*

A BEGINNING POINT FOR MEASUREMENT

Efforts to measure student engagement are just beginning.[7] The Center for Leadership in School Reform (CLSR), a nonprofit corporation I founded in 1988, has recently engaged in a partnership arrangement with software development firm Tetra-Data that is intended to create ways of collecting and managing data relevant to engagement that will be unobtrusive, require little additional teacher effort, and be easy to manage and analyze. However, no standard measures exist now. Therefore, principals and teachers, while taking advantage of what is provided here, need to be prepared to create their own measures. The following observations are important as foreground to this creative effort:

- Each of the five types of engagement should be treated as a discreet category rather than a point on a continuum. For example, it should not be assumed that the student who is authentically engaged in the task assigned is more engaged than the student who is ritually engaged. The authentically engaged student is simply engaged in a different way. Similarly, the passively compliant student is not less engaged than the ritually engaged, even though passive compliance is likely to produce less effort than is either ritual engagement or authentic engagement.[8]

- Retreatism is really a form of disengagement, which is categorically different from engagement.

- Rebellion is—or may be—a form of engagement, but the focus of the engagement may be at odds with that which is needed if the student is to learn what it is intended he or she learn. The student who cheats on a test, for example, may be authentically engaged in doing what is needed to get a good grade but rejects completely the requirements of the tasks he or she needs to complete to accomplish this end by legitimate means.

RUBRICS

Rubrics are often useful in developing ways of measuring social phenomena. The five rubrics that follow can serve as frameworks for teachers and principals who are working toward developing ways of assessing student engagement:

- *Authentic engagement.* Authentically engaged students see meaning in what they are doing, and that meaning is connected to ends or results that truly matter to the students. Indeed, these authentically engaged students may be willing to do some boring and otherwise meaningless tasks, precisely because they see the linkage between what is being done and some task-related end of significant consequence to them. For example, students who want to become musicians regularly practice scales (not a particularly exciting task) because they see such practice as a means of achieving the end they have in view.

Authentically engaged students see meaning in what they are doing.

The critical point is that when students are authentically engaged, the distinction between ends and means becomes blurred. What in another context they would consider trivial and meaningless becomes loaded with meaning and significance to those who are authentically engaged. Thus, the student who diligently proofreads his or her paper to ensure that the grammar and punctuation are correct because he or she takes pride in being a good writer is engaged in a different way from the student who does such checking only "when it counts for a grade."

- *Ritual engagement.* This form of engagement is typified by the separation of means from ends. Students do the work and carry out the tasks, sometimes with diligence and persistence, but they do so for reasons that are disassociated from the task itself. The end toward which the task is directed (such as the production of a good work product) is unimportant to the student. What is important is the impact the successful completion of the task will have on other areas of school life or on the student's personal life. Thus a student who is bent on being admitted to a highly selective college is more likely to be concerned with the grade she or he receives in the course than with whatever learning must be done to attain that grade. "Tell me what to do and I will do it, no matter how meaningless it is to me," characterizes a ritual response.

• *Passive compliance.* As the word *compliance* indicates, passive compliance suggests acceptance and resignation more than enthusiasm and commitment. When students respond in a passive compliant mode, they are seeking minimums. What does it take to get by here? is a more likely question than is, What do I need to do to excel? Minimums and accommodations are more important than accomplishment and attainment.

  Passive compliance suggests that students are engaged but, like ritual engagement, the ends and the means are separated. Furthermore, passive compliance suggests that students find little of value associated with the task either directly or indirectly. Passive compliance is more likely motivated by a student's desire to avoid unpleasant consequences than by the pursuit of some positive value or goal.

• *Retreatism.* Retreatism carries with it the suggestion of disengagement. The task or assignment has no attraction to the student, and the student is not compelled by other considerations, such as the need for a passing grade, athletic eligibility, or peer approval, to do anything active to support the task. Retreatism suggests a type of withdrawing of support for the activity that is taking place or is expected to take place. However, students who are adapting to a task by retreating from its demands do not substitute their own agenda into the situation. They simply withdraw—mentally and sometimes physically—from what is going on in the immediate environment.

• *Rebellion.* Students responding by rebelling overtly reject the task, refuse to comply, and often lack willingness to be passive about the failure to comply. Indeed, rebellion can involve seeking to get a desired end by substituting new, and disapproved, means, such as cheating, negotiating standards, or bringing parental pressure to bear.

OBTAINING RELEVANT DATA

The way to go about getting relevant data depends on the context. Assessing engagement in a primary school requires different strategies than will be needed in a high school. If the level of trust among faculty is high, one set of strategies may work, but if trust is low, other strategies will need to be developed. In general, however, in the early stages, it is probably wise to avoid focusing on individual classrooms unless the teachers volunteer to submit their classrooms to such public scrutiny. Lacking a significant number of volunteers, it seems better to focus attention on the school in general.

One way of doing this is for the principal to administer to all students a questionnaire like the one presented in Exhibit 1.1. Using the data from this questionnaire—or some variation thereof—it is possible to construct a pie chart showing the pattern for the week. This exercise could be repeated for several weeks to see if

---

**Exhibit 1.1.
Student Questionnaire on Classroom Engagement.**

Looking back over the past week, which of the following statements most closely reflects the way you have approached your classes and the work your teachers have assigned? (Circle the statement that most closely reflects your view.)

- I really have been engaged in the work and in my classes, and I generally do what I am asked to do because I see the relevance of what I am being asked to do to things that I care about. [authentic engagement]

- I always pay attention in class and do the work I am assigned because I want to get good grades, but I really don't see much merit in what I am asked to do and would not do it if I did not feel I had to. [ritual engagement]

- I do what I need to do to get by, but I really don't put out any more effort than I feel I have to if I am to stay out of trouble. [passive compliance]

- I am bored, and I have done very little work for my classes, but I have not caused any trouble for my teachers. [retreatism]

- I have been in some trouble because I have not done what the teacher wants me to do, but that is just the way it goes. I don't plan to change what I am doing. [rebellion]

---

there is any variation. Making such data public in the teachers' lounge will undoubtedly do much to focus attention on issues related to engagement. (It is important that no effort should be made to identify individual teachers or isolate individual classrooms. In the early stages, teachers need the protection of anonymity.)

Another strategy is to create an interview protocol that teachers or the principal might use that calls on students to express their feelings about their responses to their classes in general or to the class of a particular teacher. The results of these interviews might then be reviewed by a teacher or group of teachers and categorized into one of the five categories of engagement listed above. (Here, the rubrics provided should be instructive.) This process has the advantage of encouraging teachers to reflect on the meaning of each category but the disadvantage of making responses public, which can be threatening to both the students and the teachers involved.

Experience indicates that as principals work with teachers on these issues, the threat value of interviews decreases, especially as teachers begin to see how such data can be of use to them in determining the effects and effectiveness of what they are doing on a daily basis. The principal should not, however, force anyone to participate in this process. Rather, he or she should seek out those "trailblazers and pioneers" (see Schlechty, 1997) on the faculty who might find such an adventure exciting as well as productive. Teachers who want to initiate such an activity should solicit the support and involvement of the principal, even as they are testing out some of these ideas on their own.

A CAUTION

The idea of the teacher as performer, rather than the teacher as leader and inventor, creates conditions that sometimes have unfortunate consequences; for example, when teachers view themselves and their own performance as the central concern, they sometimes see the lack of authentic engagement in their classrooms as a reflection on themselves and their personality. They also see the quest for evidence regarding such matters as a prelude to one more effort to "work on the teacher."

What the committed principal and trailblazer teachers must communicate to those who are reluctant to participate is that trying to work on a teacher to make him or her more engaging has proved to be just about as productive of improved student performance as has the effort to work on the students. It is time to quit this futile effort and work on something that really matters: the quality of the work provided to students. If teachers can control the quality of the work they assign students, there is some prospect of increasing student engagement. If students become engaged in the right "stuff," they are likely to learn what we want them to learn. When students learn what it is intended that they learn, we will have schools that have done what they are supposed to do.

Notes

1. The idea or ritual engagement, as well as the ideas of retreatism and rebellion, were suggested to me by Robert K. Merton's book *Social Theory and Social Structure* (1968).

2. This does not mean I advocate abandoning authentic engagement as a goal. Rather, I make this observation to point out that teachers can experience the illusion of success by having a well-managed classroom where ritual engagement and passive compliance are the norm and never really create an environment where authentic engagement is the norm. That is why I insist on distinguishing between the well-managed classroom and the highly engaged classroom.

3. Alfie Kohn has made this point repeatedly (see, for example, Kohn, 2001), as have others.

4. Some empirical research supports this view. See, for example, Kohn's discussion (2001) of the relationship between superficial coverage and test scores. See also *"Doing School": How We Are Creating a Generation of Stressed Out, Materialistic, and Miseducated Students* (Pope, 2001) and *Another Planet: A Year in the Life of a Suburban High School* (Burkett, 2001). The authors of these books make a powerful case that much that passes for academic excellence in even the best of schools is little more than ritual engagement or passive compliance. Cheating, which is a form of rebellion, also appears to be more common that one might want to believe.

5. Outside observers, as well as some teachers, sometimes confuse activity with engagement. Activity of the hands-on variety can be an effective means of increasing engagement, but some types of hands-on activity are mindless and without meaning or significance. Engagement has to do with the extent to which an activity has meaning and significance to the student rather than the amount of physical effort expended. It is therefore important to focus attention on the meaning the work has for students rather than the amount of "activity" involved.

6. The Center for Leadership in School Reform has developed a two-day

workshop intended to develop the needed level of awareness among school faculties. I strongly urge interested principals to contract for this service. Absent that, I would encourage principals to obtain the training materials from CLSR and participate in a CLSR principal training program intended to develop the skills needed to conduct such a workshop on site.

7. A wide body of research deals with time on task. Readers should not assume that the measurement problems associated with assessing patterns of engagement can be solved in the same way as those who have tried to measure time on task. *Time on task* and *engagement* are not synonyms. Observational studies may help assess engagement, but any reasonable assessment of patterns of engagement will involve some sort of direct and focused responses from individual students; thus interviews and questionnaires will probably be required as well as observation.

8. The idea that different types of engagement produce different levels of effort, combined with the idea that effort and learning are associated, suggests some intriguing research possibilities.

The WOW School

In a WOW school, nearly all classes are highly engaged, and when they are not, teachers make every possible effort to redesign the pattern of activity in the classroom so that more students are authentically engaged.

Beliefs shape visions, and visions drive missions. Visions are not accomplished; they are realized. Missions are sets of goals that must be accomplished for visions to be realized (Schlechty, 1997).

Beliefs shape visions, and visions drive missions.

Beliefs are statements on which one is willing to act. For example, one of the beliefs on which the WOW framework is based is that teachers are leaders and inventors. Those who accept the WOW framework are saying implicitly that they are willing to act on the assumption that this assertion is—or should be—so.

From Vision to Reality

- Beliefs serve as the basis for visions.
- Visions shape missions and strategic goals.
- Missions set strategic goals.
- Strategic goals indicate needed actions.
- Action goals define tasks and specify activity.

Given a belief or set of beliefs, it then becomes important to ask, "What would that part of the world that my beliefs address look like if these beliefs were acted on?" The result will be an idealized picture of a desired—though yet to be realized—state of being. Such a picture is, or can be thought of as being, a vision.

IDENTIFYING MISSIONS

By assessing how closely current reality comes to satisfying the conditions suggested by the vision, it is possible to begin to conceive of strategies for moving reality and vision more closely together. These strategies, when they come together in a set of goals, are commonly referred to as missions. Strategic goals are therefore missions that have been unbundled. Action goals are strategic goals that have been made operational, or actionable. It is by assessing current reality in relationship to vision that strategic goals are set, and it is by making strategic goals operational and actionable that action goals can be derived. In summary, beliefs serve as the basis for visions, visions shape missions, missions set strategic goals, and strategic goals indicate needed actions.

THE WOW SCHOOL: A VISION

What would a school look like if the beliefs asserted in the Introduction were the basis for action in it or in the school district? Although the local context will surely determine the way these beliefs will be manifest in specific terms, there are some general conditions that would certainly be in evidence. The following are among the things one would be likely to find in a school where Working on the Work is deeply embedded in the culture:

Standard 1: Patterns of Engagement. Nearly all classes are highly engaged, and when they are not, teachers make every possible effort to redesign the pattern of activity in the classroom so that more students are authentically engaged.

Standard 2: Student Achievement. Parents, teachers, the principal, and the board of education, as well as others who have a stake in the performance of the schools, are satisfied with the level and type of learning that are occurring.

Standard 3: Content and Substance. Teachers and administrators have a clear, consistent, and shared understanding of what students are expected to know and to be able to do at various grade levels. This understanding is consistent with such official statements of expectations as state standards and standards established by local boards. Teachers and administrators also have a reasonable assessment of student interest in the topics suggested by these expectations and standards.

Standard 4: Organization of Knowledge. Teachers and support personnel (for example, media specialists) generally endeavor to ensure that the media, material, books, and visuals used to present information, propositions, ideas, and concepts to students are organized in ways that are most likely to appeal to the personal interests and aesthetic sensibilities of the largest possible number of students and to ensure as well that students have the skills needed to use these materials.

Standard 5: Product Focus. The tasks students are assigned and the activities they are encouraged to undertake are clearly linked in the minds of the teacher *and* the students to performances, products, and exhibitions about which the students care and on which students place value.

Standard 6: Clear and Compelling Product. When projects, performances, or exhibitions are part of the instructional design, students understand the standards by which these projects, performances, or exhibitions will be evaluated. They are committed to these standards and see the real prospect of meeting the stated standards if they work diligently at the tasks assigned and are encouraged.

Standard 7: A Safe Environment. Students and parents feel that the school as well as each classroom is a physically and psychologically safe place: success is expected and failure is understood as a necessary part of learning, there is mutual respect between and among faculty and students, and the fear of harm or harassment from fellow students and demeaning comments from teachers is negligible.

Standard 8: Affirmation of Performances. Persons who are significant in the lives of the student, including parents, siblings, peers, public audiences, and younger students, are positioned to observe, participate in, and benefit from student performances, as well as the products of those performances, and to affirm the significance and importance of the activity to be undertaken.

Standard 9: Affiliation. Students are provided opportunities to work with others (peers, parents, other adults, teachers, students from other schools or classrooms) on products, group performances, and exhibitions that they and others judge to be of significance.

Standard 10: Novelty and Variety. The range of tasks, products, and exhibitions is wide and varied, and the technologies that students are encouraged to employ are varied as well, moving from the simplest and well understood (for example, a pen and a piece of paper) to the most complex (for example, sophisticated computer applications).

The WOW School

Standard 1: Patterns of Engagement. Nearly all classes are highly engaged, and when they are not, teachers make every possible effort to redesign the pattern of activity in the classroom so that more students are authentically engaged.

Standard 2: Student Achievement. Parents, teachers, the principal, and the board of education, as well as others who have a stake in the performance of the schools, are satisfied with the level and type of learning that are occurring.

Standard 3: Content and Substance. Teachers and administrators have a clear, consistent, and shared understanding of what students are expected to know and to be able to do at various grade levels. This understanding is consistent with such official statements of expectations as state standards and standards established by local boards. Teachers and administrators also have a reasonable assessment of student interest in the topics suggested by these expectations and standards.

Standard 4: Organization of Knowledge. Teachers and support personnel (for example, media specialists) generally endeavor to ensure that the media, material, books, and visuals used to present information, propositions, ideas, and concepts to students are organized in ways that are most likely to appeal to the personal interests and aesthetic sensibilities of the largest possible number of students and to ensure as well that students have the skills needed to use these materials.

Standard 5: Product Focus. The tasks students are assigned and the activities they are encouraged to undertake are clearly linked in the minds of the teacher *and* the students to performances, products, and exhibitions about which the students care and on which students place value.

Standard 6: Clear and Compelling Product. When projects, performances, or exhibitions are part of the instructional design, students understand the standards by which these projects, performances, or exhibitions will be evaluated.

Standard 11: Choice. What students are to learn is usually not subject to negotiation, but they have considerable choice and numerous options in what they will do and how they will go about doing those things in order to learn.

Standard 12: Authenticity. The tasks students are assigned and the work they are encouraged to undertake have meaning and significance in their lives now and are related to consequences to which they attach importance.

They are committed to these standards and see the real prospect of meeting the stated standards if they work diligently at the tasks assigned and are encouraged.

Standard 7: A Safe Environment. Students and parents feel that the school as well as each classroom is a physically and psychologically safe place: success is expected and failure is understood as a necessary part of learning, there is mutual respect between and among faculty and students, and the fear of harm or harassment from fellow students and demeaning comments from teachers is negligible.

Standard 8: Affirmation of Performances. Persons who are significant in the lives of the student, including parents, siblings, peers, public audiences, and younger students, are positioned to observe, participate in, and benefit from student performances, as well as the products of those performances, and to affirm the significance and importance of the activity to be undertaken.

Standard 9: Affiliation. Students are provided opportunities to work with others (peers, parents, other adults, teachers, students from other schools or classrooms) on products, group performances, and exhibitions that they and others judge to be of significance.

Standard 10: Novelty and Variety. The range of tasks, products, and exhibitions is wide and varied, and the technologies that students are encouraged to employ are varied as well, moving from the simplest and well understood (for example, a pen and a piece of paper) to the most complex (for example, sophisticated computer applications).

Standard 11: Choice. What students are to learn is usually not subject to negotiation, but they have considerable choice and numerous options in what they will do and how they will go about doing those things in order to learn.

Standard 12: Authenticity. The tasks students are assigned and the work they are encouraged to undertake have meaning and significance in their lives now and are related to consequences to which they attach importance.

FRAMING THE DIALOGUE

Two types of dialogues must go forward if a school culture is to be transformed into a culture that supports Working on the Work as "the way we do business here." First, internal dialogue must occur as each person talks to himself or herself about his or her own situation, own role, and personal views regarding these matters; this is *dialogue as personal reflection.* The second form of dialogue involves conversations between and among individuals and groups. Sometimes these conversations are between peers and sometimes between a teacher and a principal. Sometimes these conversations involve only two people; sometimes the entire faculty is involved.

Generally, such conversations are much more productive when they are disciplined by a common set of questions. Such questions can provide focus and direction to what is being discussed. Indeed, without such questions, what promises to be a dialogue can become an argument where rhetoric more than reality and opinion more than fact become the currency of the realm.

Disciplined conversations will help move a school from words to action.

The questions that follow have proved useful in helping faculties begin the conversations that must begin if Working on the Work is to move from interesting words and slogans to a program of action.[1]

Standard 1: Patterns of Engagement. Nearly all classes are highly engaged, and when they are not, teachers make every possible effort to redesign the pattern of activity in the classroom so that more students are authentically engaged.

- Are most students, most of the time, authentically engaged in the tasks they are assigned?

- Do teachers intentionally plan the work they provide to students in ways that reflect attention to building in those qualities that show the most promise of increasing authentic engagement?

- When the pattern of student engagement differs from that which teachers want or expect, do teachers analyze the work provided to discover what might account for the difficulty, or do they instead seek first to explain away the lack of engagement as due to factors beyond their control?

- Do teachers commonly work together to analyze the characteristics of the work they are providing students? Do they provide each other with assistance and advice regarding ways of making the work more engaging to students?

- Is there evidence that over time, the level of authentic engagement has increased and the amount of rebellion, retreatism, and passive compliance have decreased?

Standard 2: Student Achievement. Parents, teachers, the principal, and the board of education, as well as others who have a stake in the performance of the school, are satisfied with the level and type of learning that are occurring.

- Are there solid data on which to base judgments regarding student achievement?

- Are the data available sufficient to persuade those who need to be persuaded (parents, teachers, community leaders, state officials) that they have an accurate picture of the level of student achievement in the school?

- Are parents satisfied that their children are progressing as they believe they should progress and learning what they need to learn?

- Are those who "receive" students from the school (middle schools in the case of elementary schools, high schools in the case of middle schools, institutions of higher education and employers in the case of high schools) satisfied that students from the school are learning what they need to learn to succeed in their environment?

- Do students who have attended the school believe that they learned what they needed to learn while in attendance? Do they have an overall favorable judgment of the quality of their experience in the school?

Standard 3: Content and Substance. Teachers and administrators have a clear, consistent, and shared understanding of what students are expected to know and to be able to do at various grade levels. This understanding is consistent with such official statements of expectations as state standards and standards established by local boards. Teachers and administrators also have a reasonable assessment of student interest in the topics suggested by these expectations and standards.

- Can teachers and principals articulate what students under their tutelage are expected to know and to be able to do?

- Are teachers and the principals in agreement regarding what students are to be expected to know and be able to do?

- Do the ideas, propositions, and facts that are presented or made available to students reflect the best understandings of experts in the field of concern? Are they consistent with the views and lines of argument presented by scholars in the relevant disciplines?

- Have the faculty and the principal conducted a careful review of standardized tests (local and state sponsored) to determine the content students are expected to master?

- When the faculty is in disagreement with the official standards used to assess student performance, do they make their views known to the officials who have promulgated them, as well as to parents and others who are in a position to influence such decisions?[2]

- Do the teachers provide students with a wide range of activities that call on them to work with content and processes that have been identified as worth knowing and worth mastering?

Standard 4: Organization of Knowledge. Teachers and support personnel (for example, media specialists) generally endeavor to ensure that the media, material, books, and visuals used to present information, propositions, ideas, and concepts to students are organized in ways that are most likely to appeal to the personal interests and aesthetic sensibilities of the largest possible number of students and to ensure as well that students have the skills needed to use these materials.

- Do most teachers clearly take student interests into account when developing units of work, creating tasks, or designing assignments?

- Are classroom teachers aware of the fact that some students find the content uninteresting, and do they attempt to compensate for this fact by embedding this content in activities, tasks, and assignments that engage the students who are not interested in the subject?

- If student interest in the subject or content is low, are teachers more attentive to designing high-interest activities than when student interest in the content is high?

- Are curriculum materials available that will support students' working on and with the concepts, facts, skills, understandings, and other forms of knowledge it is expected they will deal with, understand, and master?

- Do teachers employ a wide range of media and presentation formats to appeal to students with different learning styles and ways of thinking?

- Is the content presented rich? That is, as much as is possible and practical, are students called on to conduct experiments, read primary source materials, and read books and articles that convey powerful ideas in a powerful way?

- When students are assigned to read a book, use a computer, or employ some other means to acquire information, do teachers ensure that students have the skills to use these technologies?

- When discussions occur, are they disciplined with facts and the rules of logic?

- Are serious efforts made to cause students to use what they are learning to analyze problems, issues, and matters of concern to them?

- Are serious efforts made to encourage students to develop an interdisciplinary perspective, for example, to see how what they are learning in a history class might have relevance for what they are learning in mathematics, language arts, and other subjects?

Standard 5: Product Focus. The tasks students are assigned and the activities students are encouraged to undertake are clearly linked in the minds of the teacher *and* the students to performances, products, and exhibitions about which the students care and on which students place value.

- Do teachers systematically assess students' interests to determine the kinds of products that will be of interest to the students?

- Is the work teachers assign often linked to a product, performance, or exhibition?

- Do students see a clear connection between what they are doing and what they are expected to produce?

- Do teachers endeavor to personalize products so that different student interests are responded to while students are engaged in what is otherwise the same activity? For example, are students who have a high need for affiliation accommodated at the same time that students with a strong need for independence and novelty are accommodated and responded to?

- Do students generally place personal value on the products and performances they are asked to produce?

Standard 6: Clear and Compelling Product. When products, performances, or exhibitions are part of the instructional design, students understand the standards by which these products, performances, or exhibitions will be evaluated. They are committed to these standards and see the real prospect of meeting the stated standards if they work diligently at the tasks assigned and are encouraged.

- Do students clearly understand the standards by which their performances, products, and exhibitions will be assessed?

- Do the students find the standards used to assess their work relevant, meaningful, and important to them, or do they view these standards as personally irrelevant conditions that they must meet to satisfy the needs of the teacher or the system?

- Are students encouraged to assess their own work in terms of the standards set, and do they participate frequently in group assessment processes?

- Do teachers routinely hold assessment conferences with individual students or small groups of students for the purpose of assessing the quality of student products?

- Is student success in creating a product that meets the specified standard the primary goal of assessment, or is the goal of assessment to justify the distribution of rewards and grades?

- Is timeliness treated as a condition of work rather than as a goal or a standard? For example, do teachers place more emphasis on the quality of the product than they place on the amount of time required to produce it?

- Are peer evaluation and public discussions of performances, exhibitions, and products commonplace in the classroom and in the rest of the school?

Standard 7: A Safe Environment. Students and parents feel that the school as well as each classroom is a physically and psychologically safe place: success is expected and failure is understood as a necessary part of learning, there is mutual respect between and among faculty and students, and the fear of harm or harassment from fellow students and demeaning comments from teachers is negligible.

- As measured by such things as the number of discipline referrals, acts of violence, and threatening behavior, are the school and each classroom an objectively safe environment?

- Do students and teachers feel that they are as safe as can be in the school?

- Do the faculty and the administration treat each other with respect and deference? For example, are conversations and discussions in the teachers' lounge and faculty meetings friendly and civil, or are they characterized more by hostility, snide remarks, and generally discourteous behavior?

- Do faculty members treat students with respect?

- Are students respectful of each other, faculty members, and other adults in the school?

- When students interact, for example, in peer evaluations, are the interactions respectful, friendly, and supportive?

- When students fail to meet standards but are making sincere efforts, do the teacher and the student accept the failure as a normal part of the learning process, or are nearly all failures to meet standards responded to with negative comment and sanctions?

- Are sincere efforts being made to ensure that students have access to the resources needed (people, time, and technologies in particular) to provide optimum opportunities for success?

- When failures occur, do the teacher or other adults work directly with the student to diagnose the cause of the failure and correct the situation?

- When a student (or group of students) fails to meet standards after numerous tries, do faculty members work together to find new approaches to the task?

Standard 8: Affirmation of Performances. Persons who are significant in the lives of the student, including parents, siblings, peers, public audiences, and younger students, are positioned to observe, participate in, and benefit from student performances, as well as the products of those performances, and to affirm the significance and importance of the activity to be undertaken.

- Are students, individually and in groups, provided opportunities to display for others what they are doing in class and in school? For example, are sixth-grade students writing stories for second graders?

- Are parents and guardians invited into the standard-setting process for students, and do they function as full partners in the evaluation of the students' performance in school and in the classroom?

- Do adults other than parents, teachers, and guardians regularly view student performances and products and comment on what they see?

- Is the work students are assigned designed in a way that clearly communicates that the effort each student expends is important not only to his or her learning and to himself or herself, but also to the functioning of the group and the needs of others who are significant to the student?

Standard 9: Affiliation. Students are provided opportunities to work with others (peers, parents, other adults, teachers, students from other schools or classrooms) and classrooms on products, group performances, and exhibitions that they and others judge to be of significance.

- Does classroom and out-of-classroom work often involve two or more students working together on a common product?

- Is group work designed in such a way that cooperative action is needed to complete the work assigned successfully, or could the work be accomplished by one person working alone?

- Are students frequently given work to do that requires them to work with parents and other adult members of the community (including senior citizens) to complete tasks and assignments?

- Are some of the products students produce clearly intended to be useful to other students, parents, or community leaders?

- Do students know enough about group processes to analyze and evaluate the operation of their own groups?

- Is electronic technology (for example, the Internet) used to build cooperative networks among students, as well as between students and adult groups?

Standard 10: Novelty and Variety. The range of tasks, products, and exhibitions is wide and varied, and the technologies students are encouraged to employ are varied as well, moving from the simplest and well understood (for example, a pen and a piece of paper) to the most complex (for example, sophisticated computer applications).

- Do teachers employ a wide range of formats and varied modes of presentation?
- Are all students provided opportunities to lead others, and are they provided assistance in carrying out leadership functions when they have difficulty?
- Is the setting for instruction varied, or does all instruction occur in a classroom?

Standard 11: Choice. What students are to learn is usually not subject to negotiation, but they have considerable choice and numerous options in what they will do and how they will go about doing those things in order to learn.

- Are students provided opportunities to select modes of presentation and means of acquiring information?
- Are students provided opportunities to participate in decisions regarding the processes to be employed in assessing performance and determining the standards by which their performance will be evaluated?
- Are the technologies available to teachers and students varied (ranging from pencils to sophisticated computer programs, presentation technologies, laptop publishing, and so on)?
- Do teachers and students know how to use the technologies available to them, and is easy access ensured?
- Do students and teachers feel that they have significant control over their own destiny in the school and the classroom, or do they feel relatively powerless?

Standard 12: Authenticity. The tasks students are assigned and the work they are encouraged to undertake have meaning and significance in their lives now and are related to consequences to which they attach importance.

- Does the quality of products, performances, and exhibitions have consequences for the student about which the student cares?
- Do students feel that the tasks they are assigned are within reach if they expend the effort?

- Are tasks designed in ways that increase student ownership for the quality of the results?

- Are the consequences of meeting standards and failing to meet standards known to the students, and do they understand that meeting them is important to their current circumstances, as well as to future prospects?

- Is the work students are assigned designed in such a way that students have a positive stake in, and care about, the success of other students? Or is the work designed to make the success of one student a contributor to the failure of another (such as grading on the curve)?

STARTING THE CONVERSATION

There is no single prescription for the way the needed dialogues might occur in a school or within the private reflections of the individual teacher. I am persuaded, however, that until and unless such dialogues do occur, and until they proceed on a systematic basis, there is little chance that the power of Working on the Work can be fully realized.

One way a faculty might begin this process is each month to take up one of the dialogue topics in the WOW vision and its related questions and assign responsibility to different faculty members, or teams of faculty members, for developing a data-based answer to each of the questions listed.[3] The questionnaire provided in Appendix A is intended to be used both by principals interested in developing a profile of the operating style of the school they are assigned to lead and by faculty members who are interested in working with a principal to develop a collective view of the school. Such a collective view is essential if useful school improvement plans are to be developed. The scheduled faculty meeting could provide a forum for reporting on conclusions, discussing their accuracy, and considering possible implications for action.

Another way a faculty might proceed is for each faculty member to complete the questionnaire provided in Appendix B and then use a summary of these responses as the basis for faculty discussions. If this is done, the distribution of responses (the number or percentage in each of the five response categories) will be more useful than some mean score or average. The intent of the conversation should be to reveal areas where there is consensus and areas where there is disagreement and to seek consensus based on arguments that can be supported by data. Distributions of responses are most useful in the pursuit of such a goal.

The individual teacher, perhaps using the questionnaire presented in Appendix B as a guide, could set about systematically examining the operation of his or her own classroom. In the course of this examination, the teacher might want to interview students or perhaps even develop and administer a questionnaire to students.[4]

Individual teachers might want to supplement their own observations, which may be distorted by some level of initial defensiveness, by inviting colleagues to complete the questionnaire provided in Appendix B. And as experience is gained, the principal might be invited to complete such a questionnaire as well.[5]

DISCIPLINED DIALOGUE

To make conversations about engagement and patterns of classroom operation most productive, principals and teachers probably need to pursue answers in a somewhat systematic way. This does not mean that they need to go down the list and answer each question in order, although as a guide to private reflection, this might not be a bad idea. What they do need to do is understand that all of these questions deserve attention. The answers to some questions will be so obvious that little time will need to be spent on the question. For others, it may be necessary to spend considerable time finding data on which to base whatever answers there are to be found.

Here, a word of caution is in order: sometimes the obvious answer is not the most accurate answer. For example, teachers sometimes overestimate the amount of authentic engagement in their classroom and sometimes even see retreatism as a form of passive compliance. If teachers really want to understand the patterns of engagement in their classroom, they are going to have to learn to ask students about these matters. Such matters cannot be understood through casual observation. Systematic interviews and probing discussions are required.

Sometimes the obvious answer is not the
most accurate answer.

Similarly, the answers that one person or one role group will provide to some of these questions will be very different from the answers another person or group will provide. Some of the activities suggested previously (for example, the monthly dialogue sessions and peer observations) are intended to help reveal these differences in perceptions. In pursuing these activities, as well as in any other effort to apply the framework suggested here, it is important to keep the following in mind:

- This framework is not a lesson plan format. It is seldom the case that all of the qualities and attributes listed will be present in any given lesson, on any given day. Furthermore, some of these attributes may not be present at all. The presence of the attribute is not what is at stake here. What is at stake is student engagement. The absence of an attribute becomes an issue only when the level of student engagement differs from that which is required.

- Opinions are data, but opinions supported by additional data are better than opinions that lack such support. Thus, the principal who has a wider view of the school may see things lacking in the operation of the school that teachers, isolated in their own classroom, might not see. When this happens, some strategy needs to be developed to help the teachers gain a wider view of the school. For example, the principal might encourage teachers to shadow students or spend some time observing the work of the principal.

- Many of the data needed to answer the questions that need to be answered cannot be gained by direct observations in classrooms. To answer these questions fully, principals will need to engage teachers and students in conversation, and teachers will need to engage each other and students in conversation. Sometimes these conversations will be informal chats; sometimes they will result from formal interviews, focus group interviews, or discussions in faculty meetings.

- Once this framework is fully embraced, it will become a lens through which almost all that teachers and principals see in the school and in classrooms (their own and the classrooms of others) will be viewed. They will find themselves asking if these attributes are present, and if they are not, whether their presence would enhance the prospect of more students being more engaged and more students being taught the "right stuff." When this happens, Working on the Work has become a habit in the school.

THE ISSUE OF TIME

Activities like those described in this chapter can be very time-consuming. Sometimes the time spent may be well invested. It may sometimes be necessary, for example, to hold a one- or two-day faculty retreat in which the entire agenda is committed to ensuring a careful assessment of one or more of the sets of questions listed in this chapter.

What is important is that the principal and teachers have some confidence that they have given consideration to the issues associated with each of the questions listed previously, and where such attention is lacking, it is the obligation of school leaders to ensure that the issue is addressed.

By way of example, assume that an elementary principal, as a result of conversations with students and conversations with teachers, becomes persuaded that students are not spending much time in the study of science, and much that they are taught in the name of science is inaccurate, shallow, or otherwise suspect. Furthermore, this condition is not confined to a single classroom or to one teacher. Among the actions the principal might take are these:

- Engage the faculty in a conversation regarding the science curriculum and what they believe students need to know and be able to do at what levels.

- Encourage faculty members to compare what they say they believe children should learn to official mandates.

- When there are discrepancies between what faculty members say and official mandates, encourage discussion of why these disagreements exist. It may be, for example, that the reason for the discrepancies is that faculty members have never really been informed about the official expectations, or they have been informed but do not find these expectations either compelling or binding.

- Given the results of this discussion, encourage the faculty to work together to create a solution to the problems identified. For example, if the root of the problem seems to be that teachers have had little real exposure to science, then the faculty might want to work with a high school science department to create a summer science workshop for teachers and find ways to get high school science teachers to provide ongoing support to them as they work toward strengthening their background in science.[6]

The most critical thing to remember is that the questions outlined in this chapter are intended to provide a discipline from which principals and teachers can carry on a reasonable discourse regarding the intentions of the school faculty and the relationship between those intentions and the desires of parents and communities. Such disciplined conversations are needed if reflective discussions are to increase and meaningless babble and "happy talk" are to decrease.

Notes

1. These questions are framed in a way that focuses on school-level concerns. Individual teachers will need to adapt these questions to fit their own classrooms. The questionnaire for teachers in Appendix B, which asks teachers to reflect on their own classroom, can help in this regard. The statements in the questionnaire that are intended as descriptors are derived from the list of questions presented here.

2. The tendency of state legislators, and now the federal government, to use annual testing as the primary, if not sole, means of judging the merit and worth of the performance of students, teachers, and schools is the cause of much distress in many schools. The fact is, however, that educators who oppose such policies have not done a very good job of making their case to decision makers. If such policies are misguided, and I think they are, educators must become much more adept at the art of persuasion in the public forum than is now the case. Whining and hand wringing will not reverse a trend that has such political force behind it. Clear arguments, supported by facts, are required. Unfortunately, until the trend toward simplistic assessment is reversed, it is likely that teachers will be encouraged to settle for the more superficial forms of engagement (ritualism and passive compliance) as a matter of survival. See Kohn (2001).

3. Some will find the long list of questions too daunting to pursue each question fully. I hope these persons will accept the challenge for a full-blown analysis. Each of the questions is intended to focus attention on a slightly different dimension of the same issue. It is only when these issues are fully illuminated that a faculty, or an individual teacher, is in a position to develop truly powerful plans for improvement.

4. Some teachers may be uncomfortable with such crude measures; nevertheless, they are better than no measures at all. Over time, the measurements can be

refined, but it is well to recall that nothing can be controlled that cannot be measured, and nothing can be measured that is not understood. Understanding, measurement, and control are the keys to improvement. As understanding becomes more profound, the need for more precise measures will increase. As the need for measures increases, I have no doubt that the inventive capacity of educators is up to creating what will be needed.

5. Once the WOW framework has become deeply embedded in the culture of the school, most of the conversations between principals and teachers and among teachers would be framed around issues raised by the questions. This would mean the end of appraisal checklists and a new beginning for the idea of the principal as the principal teacher. (See Chapter Four for more discussion of this matter.)

6. On a more combative note, it might be that primary school teachers would want to quarrel officially with the notion that a formal science curriculum has any place in a primary school, other than as a base for motivating primary school students to want to learn to read. Stories about science, scientists, and astronauts—as well as dinosaurs, animals, and heroes of medicine—all have appeal to youngsters. Maybe reading these stories would do more to prepare primary school students for the adventures of science than ham-fisted efforts to teach science to children who cannot read.

Implications for Teachers

> *By exercising control over curriculum content and ensuring that the schoolwork provided is engaging, the teacher increases the probability that each child will learn what he or she needs to learn.*

Teachers are leaders, and like other leaders, they are known more by what they get others to do than by what they do themselves. Teachers are also inventors. In this role, they are called on to create schoolwork that will produce authentic engagement on the part of students. They must ensure as well that the work they create will result in their students' learning what it is intended that they learn.

The WOW framework is intended to provide teachers with discipline for the way they approach their tasks and a source of direction in the design of schoolwork. It provides a set of standards for making decisions about what might be incorporated into schoolwork to make it more likely to produce authentic engagement and desired learning. It is also useful in helping teachers assess possible sources of unwanted variance in student engagement and in creating strategies for reducing this variance.

UNDERSTANDING, ASSESSMENT, CONTROL, AND IMPROVEMENT

Improvement can occur only when the thing to be improved can be brought under control. Control is not possible without understanding. Assessment is critical to understanding.

Assessment is critical to understanding.

The logic underlying the WOW framework is straightforward. It assumes that the level and types of student learning are directly influenced by the effort students expend on tasks that call on them to learn what they are expected to learn and to practice the skills they are expected to master. The effort students are willing to expend on tasks is determined by the level and type of engagement the tasks generate. The level and type of engagement depend, in large measure, on the way the work is designed and the extent to which qualities that are built into the tasks are those that are most responsive to the needs and motives students bring to the tasks. The task of the teacher, therefore, is to design work that is responsive to student needs and motives, which result in students' learning those things it is intended they should learn.

WHAT CAN TEACHERS CONTROL?

Teachers are right when they say that there are many things that affect student learning that are beyond their control. Some of these things—the resources available, school calendars, even the level of parental involvement, for example—may be influenced by school- and district-level policymakers, but the individual teacher cannot control them. Others—for example, the emotional health of the child's family—are beyond the control of educators as a group.

This sometimes leads to frustration and special pleading. When there is evidence that a school is doing poorly or a teacher is doing poorly, the quick and easy explanation is that the problem is too many poor students in the class or too many nonsupportive parents.

Such explanations do have some validity. Clearly, students who come from affluent homes and students who have the benefit of supportive parents do have advantages. Some of these advantages cannot be offset by any amount of work by the teacher. These are societal issues that must be resolved at a societal level.

Nevertheless, there are things over which schools and teachers do exercise control that have the possibility of ameliorating some of these problems and, at the same time, improving the quality of education for *all* children, not just those who are currently doing poorly in school. Given the understandings on which the

> ### What Can Teachers Control?
>
> Teachers Can Control:
> - The content of the curriculum they actually deliver to students
> - The qualities and characteristics of the tasks assigned to students
>
> Teachers Can't Control:
> - Resources available to the classroom
> - School calendar
> - Social, economic, and family circumstances of their students

WOW framework is based, there are at least two things teachers have the real prospect of controlling:

- The content of the curriculum they actually deliver to students
- The qualities and characteristics of the tasks assigned to students

By exercising control over curriculum content, teachers ensure that each child has the opportunity to learn what it has been judged necessary for him or her to learn to be considered well educated in our society. By ensuring that the school-work provided students is engaging and requires them to work on and with the knowledge and skills they are expected to acquire and master, the teacher increases the probability that each child will learn what he or she needs to learn. The WOW framework is intended to help teachers control these matters.

KNOWING AND TEACHING THE "RIGHT STUFF"

There is no substitute for a teacher who is knowledgeable about the subject(s) he or she is trying to ensure that students learn. In the hurly-burly of school change, this obvious fact is sometimes overlooked. Too often, in the quest for improving teaching technique, the importance of the academic preparation of teachers is given scant attention. Too often, academic matters are overlooked as well in the continuing education of teachers and in conversations in the teachers' lounge. Teachers who are serious about improving what students learn in school must be just as serious about improving the state of their own intellectual development as they are about their own technical skills.

Teachers who read books and talk about them—with their colleagues as well as their students—are more likely to be imaginative about the work they design for students than are teachers who do not read and who maintain that they do not have time to do so. Teaching is more than a technical undertaking; it is an intellectual and moral undertaking. Those who teach need to have a rich intellectual life of their own if they are to inspire students to pursue academic matters with any amount of seriousness.[1]

Among the things teachers who see themselves as intellectual and moral leaders, as well as technically competent operatives, often do are these:

- Join or create study groups where serious books dealing with education issues and contemporary social and political issues are presented and discussed regularly. Kindergarten teachers profit as much from these discussions as do high school teachers. Indeed, I have found that when high school teachers and elementary teachers join the same groups, creativity is increased.[2]

- Read good novels and short stories, and listen to music, including the music their students listen to. As Deborah Meier, educator and author of *The Power of Their Ideas* (1995), has said, "The school must represent the culture it wants to encourage. If we want kids to feel that an intellectual life belongs to them, it must belong to the teachers too" (Vail, 2001, p. 22).

- Engage colleagues in serious discussions of the curriculum guide, the content of mandated tests, and other indicators of what the community expects students to know, and try to figure out what these things say about the prevailing view of what it takes to be an educated person. If they agree with the community view, they say so. If they do not, they enlist the support of colleagues and try to gain political support for their views.[3]

- They work to enrich the dialogue with parents by facilitating the creation of study groups for parents, where members discuss issues of concern and read relevant books.

- They work to be clear about what they believe regarding the ends of education and the purpose of school and engage others in conversations about those beliefs.[4]

FOCUS ON ENGAGEMENT

Student engagement should be a central concern of the teacher. Too often, this is not the case. The result is that students do not learn what they could learn if they were authentically engaged. Furthermore, the fact that students are often ritually engaged or simply compliant, rather than authentically engaged, often escapes attention. It has also been my observation that in low-performing schools, even the most effective teachers are willing to settle for passive compliance and retreatism and hope for an increase in ritual engagement rather than concerning themselves with ways of increasing authentic engagement. Given the press to improve test scores, such a response is understandable, but in the long run, it is counterproductive.[5]

In high-performing schools, especially in suburban middle schools and high schools, teachers too often settle for ritual engagement and even accept passive compliance as good enough. Indeed, the strategies they sometimes employ indicate to students that ritual engagement is all that is expected. For example, providing time to review for the test suggests that what has been learned and what will be learned is of little long-term significance, since the expectation is that it will soon be forgotten. Teaching test-taking skills emphasizes that what you can show is more important than what you know.

Certainly, test taking and test-taking skills are important. Similarly, well-conceived review sessions are not without merit. The problem is that when scores on tests and grades become more important than what is learned, much occurs that is distracting to the ends for which schools have been created. Students not only fail to learn what they need to learn to be considered well educated, but what they do learn is so shallow and vacuous that it may as well serve to lead them astray as to give them a positive direction.

Teachers therefore need to be clear-eyed about the types of engagement that typify their classroom. They need to be just as clear about what they expect in terms of engagement as they need to be with regard to expectations for what students will learn. Indeed, these two matters are so interconnected that they can never be fully separated.

The fact is, however, that engagement precedes learning. Therefore, assessing engagement is a means of ensuring the possibility of preventing deficiencies in learning. Substantial learning is not likely to occur in a classroom where most students are only compliant or are withdrawing into a retreatist mode. Ritual engagement can produce high performance on tests, but it does not produce the kind of learning that is assumed by the notion of the student as a lifelong learner.[6] Neither does ritual engagement develop the habits of mind and the habits of work that will be required if the student is to live a happy and productive life in our information-rich, knowledge-work society. Put another way, ritual engagement may produce good test scores, passive compliance may produce improved test scores—especially where retreatism and rebellion have been the norm—but real improvements can occur only as authentic engagement increases.

Real improvements can occur only as authentic engagement increases.

Among the things a teacher might do to ensure that they focus on the right things are these:

- At the end of each day, the teacher can estimate the level and types of engagement in the class and use this information in a pie chart. Over time, charts can be compared to see if there are changes or if patterns emerge.

- From time to time, the teacher interviews students or distributes a questionnaire like the one presented in Exhibit 1.1 and sees how closely what he or she believes to be the case squares with what students report.

- The teacher could invite the principal and colleagues to help assess the types of engagement that typify his or her classroom and then discuss similarities and differences in the conclusions that the observers reach.

- If the teacher does not like what he or she sees, or does like it and wants to keep it that way, he or she might try relating the patterns of engagement observed to the characteristics and qualities of the work that are the focus of the observation.

WORK ON THE WORK

To increase engagement, the processes through which variance in engagement are produced must be brought under control. Among the most important of these are the motivational processes set in motion by students' responses to the way the work is designed and to the extent to which this design is responsive to the needs and values that students bring to the situation.

The WOW framework presents attributes or qualities of schoolwork that affect these motivational processes, and by identifying them, the WOW framework encourages teachers to work on them and bring them under control. These attributes have been derived from research, theory, and empirical observations regarding the needs students bring to classrooms and the values students hold that come into play as they decide whether and how they will become engaged. In abbreviated form, these are the eight qualities:

- Product focus
- Clear product standards
- Protection from adverse consequences for initial failures
- Affirmation

- Affiliation
- Choice
- Novelty and variety
- Authenticity

The assumption of the WOW model is that teachers can choose to give emphasis to including any or all of these attributes in the work they provide students and that some students will respond favorably to some of the attributes, whereas others will respond favorably to other attributes. *It is not assumed that all of these attributes need to be present in each lesson or even in every unit.* Rather, this is a list of possibilities—things a teacher might want to consider when attempting to design work that is engaging to students and when the lessons they design turn out to be less engaging than they would like them to be.

Each of these qualities has been discussed at length in both *Inventing Better Schools* and in *Shaking Up the Schoolhouse.* The questionnaire in Appendix B is, in effect, a set of statements that operationally define these terms. Indeed, one of the uses teachers might make of this questionnaire is as a checklist for evaluating units of work they have developed or are developing and as a source of inspiration for possibilities they might otherwise overlook.

The same questionnaire, or some derivative of it, could also be used as a framework to discipline the conversation between teachers and principals and as a means of disciplining conversations among teachers as well. For example, a teacher who is having difficulty getting a high level of authentic engagement in a class might invite colleagues to provide concrete suggestions regarding ways that he or she could enhance the presence of one or more of these attributes. Or teachers who teach the same students might use the framework as a means of mutually assessing which of these attributes seem to be most important to their mutual students.

The critical point is that the framework provides a discipline, but it does so only if it is used in a disciplined way. It has been my experience that when teachers first begin to discuss what is going on in the classroom, they quickly revert to talking about what the teacher is doing and the teacher's style and manner of presentation, as opposed to the characteristics and qualities of the work the teacher has designed for students. That this should be so is understandable; most of the conversation about teaching focuses on what teachers do and sometimes on what students do. Seldom is the conversation about what the teacher intends for students to do and why it is assumed that students would voluntarily do such things.

Passive compliance can be gained through coercion. Ritual engagement can be enhanced through the enrichment of extrinsic rewards. Authentic engagement occurs only when the work is designed in a way that it appeals to values and needs that are real to the students.

The design qualities identified in the WOW framework reflect some of these values. There may be some motivating factors that have been overlooked or looked past. I am convinced, however, that teachers who use the WOW framework in a disciplined way will find that they do increase the number of students who are authentically engaged and the length of time each student is so engaged. When this happens, assuming students are engaged in the right stuff, learning will increase, and the overall performance of schools will improve as well.

THINKING AS A LEADER

To be a leader, a teacher must think as leaders do. Rather than asking, "What am I going to do?" leaders ask, "What is it that I am trying to get others to do, and what reasons might they have for doing those things?" Leaders also ask questions like, "How might I link what I want others to do to something those whom I want to follow me want, need, or value?"

To be a leader, a teacher must think as leaders do.

Perhaps the most powerful question a teacher can ask of himself or herself is, "Would my students be likely to do what I am about to ask them to do if they did not fear negative consequences for failing to do so?" If the answer to this question is no, then the best the teacher can hope for is ritual engagement and passive compliance. Authentic engagement will occur only when the tasks respond in some positive way to the motives and values students bring to the classroom. Effective leaders understand this to be so and are constantly identifying and shaping these motive forces. Effective leaders seek commitment; less effective leaders settle for compliance. Effective leaders earn attention; less effective leaders demand attendance. Teachers who understand that students are volunteers and who act on what they understand are behaving like leaders—effective leaders.

TOP DOWN AND BOTTOM UP

"Change where it counts most—in the daily interactions of teachers and students—is the hardest to achieve and the most important" (Tyack and Cuban, 1995, p. 10).[7] Like the authors of this statement, I am not pessimistic about the prospect of such reform, but I do fear that failure to advance the cause of school change more rapidly than we were able to do in the twentieth century may lead to the demise of our system of public education as a vital force in America.

There is little question that most efforts at change in the past have originated outside the classroom. The failure of such efforts has led to the idea that to be effective, reforms must come from the bottom up. That too is a dubious notion. Reforms that originate at the bottom will go nowhere if they are not taken into account, supported, and advocated from the top. Top-level administrators, including building principals, cannot make change happen, but they can suppress the effects of changes they do not support just as certainly as teachers and community leaders can sabotage any change they do not understand or endorse. That is why systemic reform—reform that is simultaneously bottom up and top down— is so essential.

*Reform needs to be bottom up
and top down simultaneously.*

The role of the teacher cannot change unless the role of the principal changes in complementary ways, and the role of the principal cannot change unless the role of the superintendent changes as well. Most important, real change in schools cannot occur as long as the way communities and parents define "real schools" reflects more their longing for the past than their anticipation of the future. It is imperative that as teachers and schools move toward real reform, faculties and school leaders find ways of ensuring that parents and key community leaders are involved and informed about what is going on and that these people are, and feel that they are, taken into account in any change that occurs.

CONSULTING WITH PARENTS

Most parents know their children much better than most teachers know them. Parents are therefore a valuable source of information for the teacher. Too often, though, teachers spend the time they have with parents telling the parent about the child. Teachers need to learn to ask parents about their children as well. Questions like, How does your child like school? What kind of assignments seem to cause him or her to show the most interest? and Why do you think this is so? can open up new avenues of insight and understanding of the needs and interest of the child.

Most parents know their children much better than most teachers know them.

Some parents may need to be taught how to observe their children and the responses their children have to the work that the teacher assigns. The time spent in

---

Questions to Ask Parents

How does your child like school?
What kinds of assignments seem to cause him or her to show the most interest?
Why do you think this is so?

---

such instruction, however, will be worth it. Parents are in a position to see and know things that no teacher, regardless of his or her expertise, can hope to know without the help of the parents. And it is on this kind of detailed knowledge that the construction of authentically engaging work must proceed.

Notes

1. The reading habits of many teachers leave much to be desired. If the intent of teachers is to be entitled to be viewed as sources of intellectual leadership in a community, then they must behave like intellectual leaders. Intellectual leaders read widely and deeply. Too many teachers fail to do this. See, for example, Howley (1995).

2. This is consistent with Margaret Wheatley's observations (1998) regarding the fact that causing people to interact who do not commonly do so has the effect of increasing creativity and the rate of innovation.

3. The January 2001 issue of *Phi Delta Kappan* contains a number of articles bearing on this point.

4. In *Shaking Up the Schoolhouse,* I distinguish between the ends of education and the purpose of schools. This is an important distinction, especially for teachers who are committed to using the WOW framework.

5. I will say more about this matter in the last chapter of this book.

6. In a recent *Phi Delta Kappan article,* Alfie Kohn (2001) cites several studies that bear on this point. Kohn's analysis, as well as the studies he cites, should be read by any group of teachers thinking about Working on the Work.

7. If I were to construct an essential reading list for teachers committed to the idea that real reform is necessary, *Tinkering Toward Utopia* by (Tyack and Cuban, 1995) would be high on the list. Also on the list would be *Left Back* (Ravitch, 2000), *Revisiting "The Culture of the School and the Problem of Change"* (Sarason, 1996), *Schoolteacher* (Lortie, 1975), and *The Sociology of Teaching* (Waller, [1932] 1967). The first two books provide a comprehensive view of the nature of reform in American education, although the authors have very different points of view. Ravitch believes that the primary reason for the shortcomings of American schools is the progressive reforms that changed the classroom. Tyack and Cuban have some doubts about the fact that these reforms ever hit the classroom with anything approaching the impact Ravitch assumes.

Sarason shows how school reform is ameliorated by the programmatic and behavior regularities of school. Lortie and Waller help us to understand better what those regularities are. In addition, the contemporary nature of Waller's description of schools, although he wrote the book over seventy years ago, helps readers to appreciate more fully the fact that schools have changed very little, though there have been many efforts to change them.

The Principal's Role

Before you can lead others, you must be clear about what you believe.

If Working on the Work is to become a habit in a school, the principal must exert strong leadership to ensure that this is the case. Lacking such leadership, it is unlikely that the ideas set forth in the preceding chapters will have any impact in any but a few classrooms, and even there, it is likely that the effort will be abandoned after a few initial tries. Working on the Work is hard work, and it requires strong support and a truly collegial environment if the habit is to survive. More than that, it requires an environment where the intentions of leaders are trusted and where it is a fact, rather than simply rhetoric, that the principal wants to work *with* teachers rather than to work *on* them.

Given a principal who is committed to this set of ideas and believes as well that his or her task is to lead rather than manage, direct rather than control, what steps might be taken to drive some of the ideas and assumptions set forth here, and in other books I have written, into the culture of the school and each classroom in that school?

BUILD OR JOIN A PRINCIPAL SUPPORT NETWORK

Principals need support, just as teachers, parents, CEOs, and children do. Support is especially critical when the principal (or any other person) is doing something that poses risks or produces uncertainty.

A principal who is committed to moving in the direction this book is intended to support is probably already involved with a group with other principals who have similar inclinations. If so, he or she should stick with it. If not, the principal should find such a group or create one if necessary.[1]

The participants of such a group should work to ensure that the group's agenda is focused on the right issues: those associated with effective leadership in knowledge work organizations. This can be done by making reading and discussions about what is read a regular part of the group activity.[2]

Care should be taken to ensure that the group does not degenerate into an "issue of the week" group, where immediate bureaucratic problems overwhelm developmental needs. (This is particularly likely to happen when all or most of the principals in the group are from the same school district.) Also, group leaders should take care to ensure that it is a problem-solving group as opposed to a complaint-sharing group. One way to do this is to organize the group around a common set of beliefs and then use these beliefs to discipline discussions and establish priorities for study and action.

GET YOUR OWN BELIEFS CLEAR

Before you can lead others on the difficult road to improved student performance, you must be very clear about what you believe about the nature of the enterprise you are trying to lead. If you determine to go down the path suggested here, it is imperative that you decide whether you can embrace and act on the assumptions stated in the Introduction to this book. Specifically, can you subscribe to the view that:

1. Students are volunteers; what they have to volunteer is their attention and commitment.
2. Differences in commitment and attention produce differences in student engagement.
3. Differences in the level and type of engagement affect directly the effort that students expend on school-related tasks.
4. Effort affects learning outcomes at least as much as does intellectual ability.
5. The level and type of engagement will vary depending on the qualities teachers build into the work they provide students.
6. Therefore, teachers can directly affect student learning through the invention of work that has those qualities that are most engaging to students.

1. Students are volunteers; what they have to volunteer is their attention and commitment.

2. Differences in commitment and attention produce differences in student engagement.

3. Differences in the level and type of engagement affect directly the effort that students expend on school-related tasks.

4. Effort affects learning outcomes at least as much as does intellectual ability.

5. The level and type of engagement will vary depending on the qualities teachers build into the work they provide students.

6. Therefore, teachers can directly affect student learning through the invention of work that has those qualities that are most engaging to students.

In addition to deciding whether you can embrace these assumptions, it is important to come to grips with what you believe about other important matters of concern to school leaders. Elsewhere, I have indicated what I believe are the most important questions leaders need to ask themselves regarding schools and schooling (see Schlechty, 1997). Developing answers to these questions is a highly personalized matter. Furthermore, the quest for a well-grounded set of beliefs to guide action is a continuous one. As for me, I believe that:

1. Every child can learn more than he or she is now learning in school *if* the child is provided with schoolwork that he or she finds to be engaging.

2. Engaging schoolwork is meaningless work unless it requires the student to acquire and use disciplined knowledge and to develop skills, attitudes, and habits of mind that give him or her access to, and a preference for, knowledge that is critically held rather than simply received.

3. Equity and excellence are mutually supportive values, and these values should always be applied to any decision made that affects life in public schools.

4. The key questions for those who are making decisions that affect schools are these: Is it just? Is it fair? Is it reasonable? Is it theoretically and empirically defensible? Is it right?

5. In a democracy, the ends of education have to do with ensuring that each child has attained sufficient mastery of reading, writing, arithmetic, and oral communication that he or she can easily access the knowledge available in the culture and can communicate to others what he or she knows or wants to know.

6. In a democracy, no child can be considered adequately educated who does not possess a basic understanding of the core academic disciplines or have a general understanding of the historic, cultural, and social forces that are shaping his or her life.

7. The purpose of school is to ensure that each student is provided with experiences that are engaging (to the student) and from which the student learns those things outlined in beliefs 3 and 4.

8. The ends of education are distinguishable from the purpose of schools. Education is a social institution that contains expressions of values and beliefs. Schools are complex social organizations that operate in the context of the educational institution to produce results that are consistent with and supportive of the institutional values being expressed.

9. For schools to serve their purposes, they must be organized around students and the needs students bring with them to school, and they must provide students with work (experiences) that responds to these needs.

10. For schools to serve their purposes, they must be transformed from their bureaucratic structure to a more customer-focused, quality-driven organization.

11. Schools and school districts are generally inept at bringing about the kind of transformational changes that are required if the schools are to serve the educational ends they must serve. Furthermore, few educational leaders seriously attend to creating the kind of conditions in their organizations that would make them adept at change.

12. The key to the survival of public education in America is the development of a cadre of school leaders who have a clear grasp of the purpose of schools: ensuring that every child, every day, is provided with engaging work to do that results in the child's learning something that is important to the child

and to the continuation of the culture. Leaders also must be skilled in creating the conditions in the systems they lead (schools and school districts) that support the changes needed to enable the schools to serve their purpose.

---

*The ends of education are distinguishable
from the purpose of schools.*

It is not my intention that readers embrace these beliefs as their own, but I hope they will give thought to them in the quest for a personal basis from which to proceed. They are the result of my own quest for meaning and thus the product of over forty years of experience that involved working with many men and women who have—or had—very well-thought-out views of how the schools of America might be improved. I hope I have learned well from them, and I hope that what I have learned is useful to readers.

INVOLVE YOUR SUPERINTENDENT AND RELEVANT CENTRAL OFFICE STAFF

I hope that many of the principals who read this book are doing so because of activity initiated by a superintendent of schools. If so, much that I will have to say in this section will be irrelevant to you. However, it has been my experience that in this age of decentralization—and even before—building principals often find ways of initiating action outside the context of official approval and support from the central office and outside the explicit knowledge of the superintendent.

Such developments have been encouraged by the fact that many principals and many school reformers have come to see the central office and the "people downtown" as more of a distraction than a help, more of a barrier to change than a resource to support it. And there are, in fact, few building principals working in school districts where there are more than eight or ten school buildings who cannot conjure up horror stories to justify the position that central office bureaucracies do sometimes get in the way of efforts to improve schools. Furthermore, there is widespread support in the literature of education for the idea that the school is the most important unit in the change process and that the position of principal is the most important position in the educational equation.

It is therefore tempting for the innovative principal and faculty to seek to isolate themselves and their school from the central office and go it alone. In fact, on more than one occasion, I have been told by principals I consider to be outstanding that the best thing the superintendent and the central office can do for them is to leave them alone to work with their faculty.[3]

As those who have invested much in school reform are beginning to discover, however, schoolhouses are inherently part of larger educational systems. The communities that affect the operation of an individual school go well beyond the community that that school can serve or can influence in any direct way. Eventually, this fact must be accommodated in any effort to bring about real improvements in schools (see Schlechty, 2000). As John Anderson (1997), head of the New American Schools Corporation, a prominent school reform organization, has observed:

> A growing body of evidence demonstrates that neither top-down system changes nor bottom-up school changes alone can lead to improvements in student achievement. What is needed is system change specifically targeted to support the improvement of classroom practice. Our experience at New American Schools bears this out and suggests that it is time we stop debating the approach, recognize that both kinds of action are necessary but not sufficient, and commit to work together to systematically apply what we know succeeds for large numbers of children in diverse communities [p. 48].

At a local level, the wise principal who decides to set on a course of action like the one suggested here will do well to make a serious effort to involve his or her local superintendent and relevant central office personnel in the effort. The time will come when their support will be needed. Change can be started at the level of the schoolhouse, but it cannot be sustained without support from the community at large. And the wise principal understands that the community his or her school serves, unless the school is in a K–12 single-school school district, is not the community at large. Rather, it is a subset of that community.

Change can be started at the level of the schoolhouse, but it cannot be sustained without support from the community at large.

The only unit that has the potential to rally the community at large behind a change, and sustain a commitment once it has been made, is the district-level unit. Furthermore, the only political unit that has the potential to exercise sustained influence over the direction of state policy is likely to be the local board of education. Therefore, the principal who is more concerned with legacy than ego will do well to work to ensure central office support, especially the support of the superintendent.

For principals who work in a school district where the agenda set forth here has yet to be embraced by the superintendent or key office staff, I offer the following advice:

- Invite the superintendent and key central office staff to join a study group of principals where relevant books and articles are discussed. Suggest that these persons lead some of the discussions using materials recommended by the study group.

- Invite one or more central office members to participate in (not lead) staff meetings and retreats where relevant reform issues are being addressed.

- Seek opportunities to get grants from local foundations and local businesses to support some of the start-up costs, and involve central office personnel and the superintendent in the quest for this funding.

- Take every opportunity to explain to the superintendent and others *why* you are doing what you are doing, as well as describing what you are doing or intend to do.

- Remember that great leaders not only lead down; they also lead up. Indeed, the real test of a leader is that he or she is able to gain support from those over whom he or she has no control and especially support from those who have the power to stop whatever it is the assumed leader wants to do.

CREATE A GUIDING COALITION

For a change to be sustained, it is essential that a group be established that can be depended on to sustain and support a course of action intended to produce change, even in the absence of the leader who initiated the change. The creation of such a group is one of the most important tasks of the principal who wants to be a change leader.

> ### *Involving the Central Office*
>
> - Invite the superintendent and key central office staff to join a study group of principals where relevant books and articles are discussed. Suggest that these persons lead some of the discussions using materials recommended by the study group.
>
> - Invite one or more central office members to participate in (not lead) staff meetings and retreats where relevant reform issues are being addressed.
>
> - Seek opportunities to get grants from local foundations and local businesses to support some of the start-up costs, and involve central office personnel and the superintendent in the quest for this funding.
>
> - Take every opportunity to explain to the superintendent and others *why* you are doing what you are doing, as well as describing what you are doing or intend to do.
>
> - Remember that great leaders not only lead down; they also lead up. Indeed, the real test of a leader is that he or she is able to gain support from those over whom he or she has no control and especially support from those who have the power to stop whatever it is the assumed leader wants to do.

In describing such groups, Kotter (1996) uses the term *guiding coalition.* There are four qualities or attributes that must be present in such groups when the group is looked at as a whole. First, there must be persons who have *power* in the organization, that is, persons who occupy positions of authority and have the ability to make things happen when the time for action is upon the group. This is one of the reasons I suggested that a wise principal will seek to involve central office staff. Many of the resources needed to support change at the building level are controlled by—or can be found by—persons in central office positions.

Second, it is essential that there be persons in the group who are *creative and have technical competence* in the area or areas that are the focus of the change. For example, if the focus of the change were in the area of curriculum, then it would be critical to have persons who possess skill in the design of curriculum materials as part of the guiding coalition.[4] Such persons should be in a position to help the team assess whether difficulties experienced in the change process are attributable to flaws in the ideas and technologies that underpin the change or whether these difficulties have more to do with the ways and means by which the change is being implemented.

Third, the presence of strong *leaders* is critical.

Finally, it is critical that the group has members who have *credibility* with those who are most likely to be affected by the change in the early stages, as well as credibility with those who are most likely to resist these changes in early stages and in later stages as well.[5]

In creating such a coalition, it is important to understand that it is not intended that this group function like a task force or a steering committee. Guiding coalitions cannot be "appointed"; they must be recruited and developed over time. Indeed, the expansion of the guiding coalition is one of the indicators that the changes intended are becoming institutionalized.

In developing the guiding coalition, the principal will need to spend a great deal of time assessing the qualities and characteristics of faculty members. Eventually, it will be necessary to make private judgments regarding the extent to which individuals clearly possess one or more of the qualities listed above. It is from among those who clearly possess the needed attributes that the initial pool of potential recruits will be found.

From among these potential recruits, the principal must then determine the extent to which they are—or can be brought to be—favorably disposed toward the kind of changes he or she has in mind. For example, when confronted with belief statements like those set forth in the beginning of this chapter, how does the teacher respond? When invited to participate in activities like those set forth in Chapters One and Two, is there a positive reaction? It is only through conversations, careful observation, and a great amount of listening that the principal—or any other leader—can make a reasonable judgment regarding those on whom he or she can depend to share an agenda and push a real effort to bring about change.

INCREASE AWARENESS

The process of building a guiding coalition requires that the principal be attentive to issues associated with raising awareness and focusing attention. Sometimes followers do not attend to what the leader wants them to attend to because the leader gives off mixed messages. Sometimes, for example, the principal says that he or she wants improved instruction but never visits the classroom, or when the classroom is visited, it is for purposes of rendering some form of evaluative judgment.

There is an old saying that "followers know what leaders expect by what the leaders inspect and what they respect." People know what leaders are "inspecting" by the questions they ask. They know what leaders respect by the answers they celebrate or endorse.

If a principal wants teachers to improve the quality of the work they are providing for students and be attentive to issues of engagement, then the questions the principal asks in the teachers' lounge, the faculty meeting, and individual conferences and conversations need to be focused on these matters. The activities suggested in Chapter One would do much to heighten teacher awareness of the importance of engagement in their classroom. Similar activities are possible with regard to the qualities of work as well.

For example, using the principal questionnaire provided in Appendix A as a guide, a principal might spend six to twelve weeks seeking data to make it possible to develop an informed judgment regarding the answers to the questions raised under each of the twelve identified attributes. In addition, the principal might encourage volunteer teachers to engage in a similar activity in their own classrooms, perhaps using the judgments of peers as well as responses from students to help them make decisions regarding their own answers. (A teacher questionnaire is provided in Appendix B.) Such activity, combined with the activity suggested in Chapter One, would almost certainly alert faculty members to the importance the principal attaches to issues related to engagement and curriculum alignment. Observing the way individual teachers respond to this set of activities will also provide data regarding who should be recruited to become members of a guiding coalition.

INVEST IN TEACHER DEVELOPMENT

As teachers come to show interest in the direction toward which the principal is pointing, it is essential that this interest be nourished. Providing interested teachers with relevant books, articles, and materials (such as access to the CLSR Web site: www.clsr.org) as well as with time for conversation and dialogue with other interested teachers and the principal as well is one way of nurturing this interest. Helping teachers enroll in workshops—perhaps districtwide workshops—aimed at creating deeper understandings of the principles underlying the WOW framework is another possibility. Perhaps the most significant action a principal can take is to work with a teacher or group of teachers to help design units of work that consciously use the WOW framework to guide the design work and to share in the responsibility of delivering that which is designed.

BE A TEACHER

The idea that the principal is—or should be—first of all a staff developer is certainly not new. Dennis Sparks, executive director of the National Staff Development Council, among others, has been advancing this notion for many years, as have I. Indeed, one of the early slogans I used when establishing the Gheens Academy in Louisville, Kentucky, around 1984 was, "Every teacher a leader, every leader a teacher, and every child a success." This is easy to say, but it is hard to do. In addition to the fact that many principals feel they do not have the time to carry out this function, many also feel that they do not have the skills.

Part of the problem principals have with becoming involved in staff development is the tendency to confuse staff development with stand-and-deliver workshops or what educators sometimes refer to as in-service. Certainly staff development involves stand-and-deliver workshops and even in-service, but it is more than that. Staff development, properly understood, includes any conscious effort on the part of leaders in a system to enhance the capacity of individuals or groups to carry out the tasks they are assigned and to pursue the goals they are expected to pursue. This means that recruitment of new employees, including teachers, is a staff development activity, just as are evaluation of performance, providing feedback, conferring with teachers, and team-building activity. Staff development is at the heart of what principals should be doing in their role of leaders of instructors.

Staff development is at the heart of what principals should be doing in their role of leaders of instructors.

When the principal walks down the hall and comments on what he or she sees, staff development is occurring. Such comments help to clarify direction, indicate priorities, and suggest alternatives. The adage presented earlier, "Followers know what leaders expect by what the leaders inspect and what they respect," is nowhere else so apt as when applied to the role of the leader as staff developer.

Sometimes the most important work conducted by the principal in the role of staff developer is helping to establish the agenda for those persons in the district, or in the school, who carry the official title of staff developer. If the principal is doing his or her job, the capacities of the staff (not just individual staff members) should be well known to him or her.

Given this knowledge, developmental needs should be easy to identify. For example, if principals are to conduct the kind of study groups suggested in Chapter Two, it is clear that there will be a need for resources to purchase books and materials. It is also likely that an outside person with skills in group facilitation might prove useful. The job of the principal in such a case would be to ensure that the appropriate central office personnel were positioned and encouraged to respond. (If there is no response from the central office or if the central office is not staffed to respond to such requests, then the superintendent has some staff development work to do as well.)

There is no escaping the fact, however, that the principal has a vital role in leading and giving creditability to formal training activities. Not all staff development activity can be delegated to staff developers. Staff development is too important to the life of the school to entrust it all to others. It is especially critical that the principal be, and be perceived by others to be, intellectually engaged and reflective about educational matters. It is also critical that formal training programs, workshops, and so on that are conducted for school staff be endorsed through the active presence of the principal, even when he or she has no active role in the activity and is already aware of what will be presented—though the intended participants may not be.[6]

FIND TIME

Most principals I have met say that they would like to do more staff development than they now do. However, many principals also say that they feel so overwhelmed by circumstances beyond their control that they simply do not have the time to give personal attention to the development of staff. Indeed, it is the perception that principals do not have time that leads many to the conclusion that try as they might, they cannot be instructional leaders. These feelings are exacerbated by state mandates aimed at increasing both site-based responsibility and site-based accountability.

There is no easy answer to such problems. It is a fact that the circumstances surrounding the role of principal sometimes make the demands of the role nearly overwhelming. It is also a fact that there is no way to invent more time and that one more time management seminar is not likely to solve the problem. What is a principal to do if he or she decides that teacher development is one of his or her primary obligations? Among the things I would suggest to the principal are these:

- Join with other principals, and do a detailed study of the way you and they use your time. Look back over six weeks and categorize your work as follows:

  1. Things I do that are clearly associated with improving instruction in my school (for example, conferences with teachers).

  2. Things I do that are indirectly but clearly linked to improving instruction (for example, conferences with parents).

  3. Things I do that have no direct bearing on instruction that are clearly im portant to the effective and efficient operation of the school or school dis trict (for example, meeting with other principals to conduct studies such as this one).

  4. Things I do for which I can see no direct payoff for either the quality of instruction or the effective and efficient operation of the school or the school district (for example, attending meetings where materials that could have been distributed electronically are transmitted orally).

- Given this list, quit doing the things in item 4. If you do them because they are mandated by the central office or by the state, join with your colleagues and approach the superintendent with your observations.

- Ask your superintendent to enlist the support of the school board and local political leaders to encourage the state to remove onerous paperwork tasks or at least justify them. If need be, write a paper describing these tasks, and show how they take you away from your real work: being an instructional leader. Ask your colleagues and the superintendent to join you in authorship. Publish your paper as an op-ed piece in the local newspaper.

- Carefully examine the items under item 3 above, and see if there are things you might consolidate, delegate, or do differently and more efficiently. For example, if you use faculty meetings to convey routine information, put the information in a memo.

- Enlist the support of the superintendent in reviewing demands placed on you by the central office staff. For example, if you feel you are too frequently at the beck and call of central office personnel, it might be possible to consolidate meetings held at the central office so that they all occur on one day.

- Look at each interaction you have with staff and with students as a training, development, and data collection opportunity. When you walk down the hall, record what you see, and later transfer (or have an assistant transfer) what you observe to some data management system. If you do not have a data management system, get one. If you have a computer, you have the capacity to have such a system.

Finding Time

- Join with other principals, and do a detailed study of the way you and they use your time. Look back over six weeks and categorize your work as follows:

  1. Things I do that are clearly associated with improving instruction in my school (for example, conferences with teachers).

  2. Things I do that are indirectly but clearly linked to improving instruction (for example, conferences with parents).

  3. Things I do that have no direct bearing on instruction that are clearly important to the effective and efficient operation of the school or school district (for example, meeting with other principals to conduct studies such as this one).

  4. Things I do for which I can see no direct payoff for either the quality of instruction or the effective and efficient operation of the school or the school district (for example, attending meetings where materials that could have been distributed electronically are transmitted orally).

- Given this list, quit doing the things in item 4. If you do them because they are mandated by the central office or by the state, join with your colleagues and approach the superintendent with your observations.

- Ask your superintendent to enlist the support of the school board and local political leaders to encourage the state to remove onerous paperwork tasks or at least justify them. If need be, write a paper describing these tasks, and show how they take you away from your real work: being an instructional leader. Ask your colleagues and the superintendent to join you in authorship. Publish your paper as an op-ed piece in the local newspaper.

- Try to get an administrative intern or seek to release, for part of each day, a teacher who aspires to be a principal to assist you with routine tasks, data collection, and data management.

- Never hold a meeting or a conference with teachers where you do not at some point cause issues related to engagement and quality work to be discussed.

- Work with central office staff developers to ensure that the programs they offer teachers in your school are aligned with your intentions and direction. When they are not, insist that changes be made. If necessary, enlist the support of the superintendent.

- Carefully examine the items under item 3 above, and see if there are things you might consolidate, delegate, or do differently and more efficiently. For example, if you use faculty meetings to convey routine information, put the information in a memo.

- Enlist the support of the superintendent in reviewing demands placed on you by the central office staff. For example, if you feel you are too frequently at the beck and call of central office personnel, it might be possible to consolidate meetings held at the central office so that they all occur on one day.

- Look at each interaction you have with staff and with students as a training, development, and data collection opportunity. When you walk down the hall, record what you see, and later transfer (or have an assistant transfer) what you observe to some data management system. If you do not have a data management system, get one. If you have a computer, you have the capacity to have such a system.

- Try to get an administrative intern or seek to release, for part of each day, a teacher who aspires to be a principal to assist you with routine tasks, data collection, and data management.

- Never hold a meeting or a conference with teachers where you do not at some point cause issues related to engagement and quality work to be discussed.

- Work with central office staff developers to ensure that the programs they offer teachers in your school are aligned with your intentions and direction. When they are not, insist that changes be made. If necessary, enlist the support of the superintendent.

The only way to get more time is to quit doing some things that are now being done, to do things differently, or to co-opt the time of others to do some of the things you now do. The list of advice for principals on time management is illustrative, not definitive. What it illustrates, however, is that the role of principal cannot be changed until principals learn to enlist the support of those who help to define that role. To change the role of principal, the superintendent must be involved, as must the central office staff, teachers, and eventually parents, boards of education, and state education agencies.

The role of principal cannot be changed until principals learn to enlist the support of those who help to define that role.

INVENTING THE FUTURE

The role of the principal is changing, and these changes are putting heavy demands on those who occupy the role—so heavy that it is becoming increasingly difficult to recruit qualified and talented people to the role (see, for example, Farkas and others, 2001). Those who are now principals have one of three choices:

- Complain about being overwhelmed, and cope with the situation until retirement.

- Quit now, and take a less stressful job.

- Work with others to redefine the role of principal so that the job can be done by ordinary men and women and so that what is done will have optimal positive effects on the lives of children, as well as on the lives of all who work in and around the school.

It is up to those who are now principals to make the role inviting to those we will need to lead our schools in the future. Much depends on the success they enjoy in this endeavor. This chapter has been written for those men and women who refuse to be victimized by the system they are in and who are committed to helping to change the system so that the quality of life of all who live in and around schools is enhanced.

Notes

1. Any principals reading this chapter who are not members of a principal support group in their own school district or geographical area might want to contact the CLSR for the names and addresses of principals who have a common interest. CLSR staff can also assist in locating opportunities to join networks.

2. CLSR offers training and support materials for such groups.

3. The charter school movement has gained considerable support because of this sentiment.

4. It is important to understand that what is being described here is not the typical task force made up of representatives of the stakeholders. The leadership team, which should be part of the guiding coalition, may decide to create such representative groups, but the function of the guiding coalition is to provide overall direction to the change effort, ensure the effort is sustained, and provide a framework for deliberation and informed debate when problematic situations arise. The guiding coalition is not, nor should it be permitted to become, an intentionally political body, nor is it representative. The guiding coalition should be a core team that can be depended on to get the job done and ensure that momentum is maintained.

5. The literature on change and innovation is replete with stories about "early and late adapters." Although I have never seen research on this matter, it has been my observation that there are early and late resisters as well. Sometimes in the early stages of change, there will be only a few persons who resist the change. In part, this is because the fact of the change is not yet well understood, and many can continue to believe that like so many prior change efforts, "this, too, shall pass." As the change becomes more evident and as its scope is more fully understood (structural and cultural change is always wide in scope), individuals begin to understand that the intended change has implications for them and for the interest groups of which they are a part. Sometimes the negative consequences of such changes—the losses—are more apparent than are the gains. This encourages a growth in resistance and the number of resisters. This is compounded by the fact that by the time a structural or cultural change has reached the point where there is a widespread

understanding that the change is real and has widespread implications, it is likely that the change has gained enough momentum within the system that the resisters will feel the need to organize a countermovement. The goal of the guiding coalition should be to enlist the support of these potential powerful resisters before they feel the need to organize a counterrevolution.

6. Over the years, I have been struck again and again by just how important the physical presence of official leaders is to the success and meaning of formal training programs. Principals attach more significance to workshops attended or led by their superintendent than they do to workshops where the superintendent is not present. Teachers too attach more meaning to workshops—especially school-based or school-oriented workshops and seminars—where the principal is present and active. There are, of course, workshops and developmental activity where this is not true. For example, teachers regularly attend university-based training programs and training programs offered by professional associations to which they attach great importance but about which their principals have little or no understanding or are totally unaware.

When attendance at such activities is encouraged, supported, and honored by the principal or the superintendent, when persons who attend such meetings are subsequently used as resources, and when the expectation that what individuals learn at such conferences is to be shared, the meaning and significance of even these activities are increased. I am sometimes appalled at the lack of accountability that some school leaders attach to attendance at some state and national conferences and meetings. Such investments should have payoff not only for the individual but for others in the system as well. Ensuring that this is so is one of the staff development functions of the principal.

The Role of the Superintendent

When the superintendent-principal relationship is strong and mutually supportive, good things can happen.

Discussions of the role of the superintendent seldom focus on the relationship between the superintendent and building principals. Even less time is spent discussing the relationship between the superintendent and individual teachers. The reason this is so is obvious. School finance, school board relationships, legal issues, community relations, and labor relations dominate the agenda for superintendents. Consequently, those who write books and conduct seminars for superintendents are more likely to attend to these topics than to the subject of superintendent-principal relationships.[1]

Yet it remains the fact that it is the relationship between the superintendent and building principals, more than any other factor, that explains the ability of school districts to ensure that change efforts are sustained beyond the tenure of the initiating principal and that whatever positive effects there are become distributed throughout the system. When that relationship is strong and mutually supportive, good things can happen. When the relationship is fragile or antagonistic, whatever improvements occur in the district will be isolated and temporary.

The relationship between the superintendent and building principals explains the ability of school districts to ensure that change efforts are sustained beyond the tenure of the initiating principal and that whatever positive effects there are become distributed throughout the system.

DEPERSONALIZATION OF RELATIONSHIPS

Most of the matters that occupy the attention of the superintendent impose themselves on the superintendent and demand a reaction. Given the other demands on schedules, it is little wonder that many superintendents, especially in large school systems, give relatively little attention to working directly with principals and with teachers.[2] Outside the context on union negotiations, principals and teachers are not positioned to demand the superintendent's attention. If such attention is to be gained, it will be necessary for the superintendent to initiate the action.

Unfortunately, many school districts are organized in ways that insulate the superintendent from meaningful and routine direct interaction with principals. For example, in large school districts, it is quite unusual for the superintendent to be regularly involved in the evaluation of the performance of principals. This task is usually delegated to one or more deputy superintendents, area superintendents, or directors. The only time the superintendent becomes involved is when disciplinary action is called for or some high-profile honor is to be bestowed.

It is equally unusual, especially in mega districts, for the superintendent to meet regularly with principals, especially in settings where significant interaction might occur (for example, in groups of fifteen to twenty principals). Even large group meetings where the superintendent is a key figure are frequently rare and ceremonial in nature.

There are, of course, many superintendents who make it a habit to visit schools and while there to engage in dialogue with individual teachers and principals. Unfortunately, too few of these superintendents routinely communicate to other principals in the district what they are seeing and hearing. Indeed, in large school systems, the fact of these visits is sometimes not known except to the relatively few principals and teachers who directly experience them. Thus the power of the visit is lost on the system generally, although it may be quite significant in the life of a particular school.

SHARED AUTHORITY VERSUS DELEGATION

Delegating authority is not the same as sharing authority. Delegating authority means to assign the right to make decisions regarding specified matters without consultation with superiors, so long as the decisions are made within the context of predetermined rules. Indeed, the primary decisions in a rationalized system that depends on delegated authority for command and control are decisions about which rules to apply. Once this decision is made, the course of action should be clear. If it is not, there is a need for more rules.

Sharing authority means that those who are entitled by their organizational position to exercise authority transmit that authority to others and empower them to exercise this authority on their behalf or in concert with them. However, the authority being exercised continues to have its locus in the office from which it is transmitted, and the occupant of that office is fully accountable for its use. Delegated authority can be assigned; shared authority can only be communicated. Delegated authority can be rationalized and impersonal; shared authority is affective and highly personalized. Delegated authority can be assigned; shared authority must be felt and believed.

By way of analogy, delegated authority operates something like a lease on a house. So long as contractual agreements are maintained, the lessee's right to privacy and personal control is protected. The landlord still owns the property but has temporarily relinquished to the lessee the right to use it.

Shared authority, on the other hand, is more like the relationship between the married couple who lives in the house. Each has his or her own identity, but the significance of the union goes beyond legal agreements. Each participates in the public identity of the other, and each gives to the other without the formal expectation of a quid pro quo (usually). The strength of the marriage is found in the tacit understandings and informal agreements that surround it more than in legal agreements. The legal agreements can be severed through divorce, but when a divorce occurs, it is likely that the tacit understandings on which the marriage was based had disappeared long before, or they never were developed and articulated.

Change requires the exercise of authority. It requires, for example, that resources be assigned or made available, including the time and talent of people, the most precious resource of all. As long as the changes are only procedural or technical, the authority needed can be assigned or delegated. A new office can be created to direct a project, and the project director can be given sufficient budgetary authority to act. However, structural and cultural change, the kind of change required by the WOW framework, requires more than changes in techniques and procedures. It requires as well changes in rules, roles, and relationships and changes in beliefs, values, commitments, and orientations.[3] This requires the exercise of moral authority. Moral authority cannot be delegated, although it can be shared. (See below and Schlechty, 1991.)

Change requires the exercise of authority.

INNOVATIONS AND SYSTEMIC CHANGE

Innovations involve new or improved ways of doing the job. Some innovations require systemic change; others do not. When systemic change is required, it is essential that the office of the superintendent be involved. The reason this is so is that systemic change deals with the moral order of the system, as well as the technical order. It redefines meanings and values, as well as procedures and processes.[4]

It is, of course, possible for technical changes to be implemented and procedural changes to be installed without the active involvement of the superintendent. It is even possible to bring about some short-term structural and cultural changes in schools without the involvement of the superintendent, although these changes are unlikely to survive the tenure of the initiating principal if they do not gain the active support and advocacy of the superintendent. The reason that this is so is that without support from authority external to the school, when it comes time for that external authority to act (for example, when resources are needed or the principal is to be replaced), the actions taken by the external authority may not be supportive of the direction that has been set by the local school faculty operating independent of the district.

A POINT OF VIEW

The role of the superintendent, whether in a small district or a large one, is a difficult one. The demands are already overwhelming. Therefore, to insist that the superintendent do yet another thing—especially to initiate other things to do—may seem like madness or ignorance. It has been my observation, however, that superintendents who give priority to finding ways of establishing and maintaining direct and vital links to building principals are much more effective at moving districtwide reform than are superintendents who rely on traditional patterns of delegation, command, and control. As I wrote in an earlier publication:

> There are two things I know about the office of superintendent. First, whatever moral authority resides in, or is bestowed upon, the school system, that authority resides in the office of the superintendent. Second, the superintendent can delegate to others nearly anything he or she wants to delegate (so long as the board consents) except the moral authority that resides in the office of superintendent. In the long run, therefore, who the superintendent is, what the superintendent values, and the style of operation supported by the superintendent will be manifest throughout the school system [1991, p. 128].

"Moral" authority cannot be delegated; it can only be shared. To bring about the kind of changes required by the WOW process, moral authority is required. That is why the personal involvement of the superintendent is so critical. It may be that a dynamic principal and committed staff can start the changes needed with nothing more than the tacit consent of the central office, but they cannot sustain the changes over time because the changes will go too deep; they will eventually challenge the basic assumption on which the school is based and the relationships between the central office and the school. Moreover, if the intent is to extend these changes beyond a single school or a small cluster of schools, the task is impossible without active support from the office of the superintendent. It requires, for example, that the superintendent endorse and legitimize what is going on in a single building as a harbinger of what he or she intends to have going on in all buildings.

This means that the superintendent will need to be willing to risk what the principal is risking. Such sharing of risks requires a great deal more trust and personal involvement than does delegation and the "plausible deniability" that delegation provides. Sharing authority assumes a personalized system and accepts the nonrational elements of emotion, affect, and personal enthusiasms as a legitimate part of the undertaking.[5]

THE WISDOM OF OTHERS

Based on over forty years of experience working with literally hundreds of superintendents, I am convinced that if the kind of change envisioned in the WOW framework is to be real, substantial, and widespread throughout a school district, the superintendent must own—and be perceived to own—the direction indicated by the change. Furthermore, it is not enough for the superintendent to endorse the change; he or she must be, and must be perceived to be, leading it.

What, then, should the superintendent do? How might the superintendent provide the kind of leadership needed and, at the same time, be sufficiently responsive to the other demands of the role to survive and thrive in what often seems a very hostile and nonsupportive environment?

It is not my intention to attempt to provide a single or definitive answer to this question. However, in my role as consultant and sometimes up-close adviser to superintendents across the United States and Canada, I have been in a relatively unique position to observe some great leaders work their way through this sort of problem. I have also learned much from studying how change leaders function in nonschool settings as well. What I have learned from these wise leaders—as well as from some who were not so wise—may be instructive to superintendents who are seeking to work out answers for themselves. Here is some of what I have learned.

Be Clear About What You Believe

It is critical that leaders be clear about what they assume and believe. Superintendents, like principals, need to take the time to examine the assumptions underlying the WOW framework and decide whether they can enthusiastically endorse them. If they cannot, they need to say so. If they can and do, they need to say so.

They also need to be clear about how these assumptions square with their personal beliefs about school. This means that they need to articulate their beliefs clearly and let what they believe be known—especially to be known by the principals on whom they must depend if what they envision is ever to be realized.

Personalize Your Relationship with Principals

Principals are the key operatives in any systemic change effort. In a well-operating system, principals are like the Roman god Janus: they look out from the school and

- Be clear about what you believe.
- Personalize your relationships with principals.
- Clarify the vision.
- Unify central staff.
- Think and act strategically.

in from the central office. It is through the principal that the direction of the district is transmitted to those inside the school.

The closer the principal is to the superintendent, the more likely the principal will be to identify personally with the direction that the superintendent supports. Therefore, the superintendent who wants to influence what goes on in schools must work to ensure a personal relationship with all the principals in the district.[6]

In operational terms, there are a number of things a superintendent can do to develop and sustain such a relationship. If you are a superintendent, you can:

- Use e-mail and invite principals to communicate directly to you. Be sure to respond within twenty-four hours to any principal's query or concern. This interaction (if you are not already doing this) will require less than an hour per day—and you can determine when that hour will be.

- Commit to meeting personally with every principal in the district for at least three hours each month in groups of no more than twenty-five.

- Put your beliefs in writing (mine are listed in the previous chapter), and ask the principals to respond to what you believe.

- Make most of the meetings you have with principals developmental meetings, not business meetings. Take the opportunity to be a teacher of the principals who work in your district. Suggest books for them to read, and then discuss these books in terms of their implications for the directions you are setting. You may want the assistance of someone who is good at designing high-quality staff development activities, but you should be the point person every time. This activity is too important to delegate, even to those to whom you have already delegated the authority to evaluate principals.

- Play a central role in whatever evaluation the principals in your district undergo. In districts with fewer than twenty principals, you should personally be involved in the evaluation of principals. In larger districts, you may need to delegate evaluative authority to others, but then you should be sure to evaluate these evaluations as part of your evaluation of those to whom authority has been delegated. Remember that people know what you expect by what you inspect and what you respect.

- Visit at least one school each week, and report to all principals, perhaps through e-mail chats, on what you see. Pick up on those things that positively reflect the direction you want to set. If there is something negative to address, deal with that in private.

- Make the induction of new principals part of your personal agenda. Have a conference of new principals in groups of no more than eight at least once each quarter for the first year and at least twice during the second year. Do not be afraid to express your hopes and dreams as well as your concerns.

Except in the largest school districts, these recommended activities should not require more than 25 percent of the time of the superintendent. For the superintendent who is committed to having an impact on the quality of experiences of students in schools, this seems a small investment. If you cannot find the time in your schedule to do these things, maybe it is time that you and your board of education consider ways of redefining your role and community expectations of that role so that you do have the time you need.

Clarify the Vision

The kind of schools envisioned in the WOW framework is described in detail in Chapter Two. But even with this detail, there is much that needs to be said to make the vision complete. Indeed, such visions are never complete; they are always in the process of becoming. For example, there is nothing said in Chapter Two regarding how the central office should relate to individual schools. There is no clear and definitive statement regarding the ends of education: what students should learn and why they should learn these things. These matters too deserve serious consideration by principals and by teachers. Only the superintendent has the moral

Personalize Your Relationships with Teachers

- Use e-mail and invite principals to communicate directly to you. Be sure to respond within twenty-four hours to any principal's query or concern. This interaction (if you are not already doing this) will require less than an hour per day—and you can determine when that hour will be.

- Commit to meeting personally with every principal in the district for at least three hours each month in groups of no more than twenty-five.

- Put your beliefs in writing (mine are listed in the previous chapter), and ask the principals to respond to what you believe.

- Make most of the meetings you have with principals developmental meetings, not business meetings. Take the opportunity to be a teacher of the principals who work in your district. Suggest books for them to read, and then discuss these books in terms of their implications for the directions you are setting. You may want the assistance of someone who is good at designing high-quality staff development activities, but you should be the point person every time. This activity is too important to delegate, even to those to whom you have already delegated the authority to evaluate principals.

- Play a central role in whatever evaluation the principals in your district undergo. In districts with fewer than twenty principals, you should personally be involved in the evaluation of principals. In larger districts, you may need to delegate evaluative authority to others, but then you should be sure to evaluate these evaluations as part of your evaluation of those to whom authority has been delegated. Remember that people know what you expect by what you inspect and what you respect.

- Visit at least one school each week, and report to all principals, perhaps through e-mail chats, on what you see. Pick up on those things that positively reflect the direction you want to set. If there is something negative to address, deal with that in private.

- Make the induction of new principals part of your personal agenda. Have a conference of new principals in groups of no more than eight at least once each quarter for the first year and at least twice during the second year. Do not be afraid to express your hopes and dreams as well as your concerns.

authority required to ensure that such difficult discussions go forward in anything but a ritual fashion.[7] Among the things a superintendent might do to promote such discussions are these:

- Meet with principals, and discuss the twelve descriptors of a WOW school set forth in Chapter Two.

- Ask each principal to work with a central office staff member to develop a profile of his or her school that provides a data-based description of the school and is responsive to the questions listed under the twelve descriptors in Chapter Two. (Principals might combine this with efforts they are undertaking with the faculty of their schools.)

- Encourage the development of a strategic plan that includes goals related to engagement and curriculum alignment, as well as goals related to student achievement.

- Encourage the development of school improvement plans that are based on assessments associated with the WOW framework.

- Require all central office staff to participate in discussions of the WOW framework and present action plans regarding ways they can provide support to building principals and teachers as they go about employing the WOW framework.

- Facilitate meetings between principals and central office during which principals review and evaluate central office plans.

- Encourage those who evaluate principals to structure their evaluation in terms that are consistent with the WOW framework.

Encourage principals to focus on engagement, curriculum alignment, and the qualities of schoolwork in their appraisals of teachers and their discussions with teachers.

Unify Central Staff

To develop sound relationships with principals, superintendents must ensure that those who work in and around the central office, especially those who are perceived by principals to have the superintendent's ear, share a common set of beliefs and a common vision. Furthermore, the superintendent must ensure that the beliefs and vision that central office staff espouse—publicly and in private conversations—are consistent with those of the superintendent. Because this matter is often not attended to, principals frequently complain of "too much centralization" when the problem is more aptly described as too *little* centralization *at the top*. For example, principals frequently complain about spending too much time at the central office in meetings. Each department head, operating independently, calls only one meeting per month, but there may be ten department heads. This occurs because the central office is not centralized rather than because the system is too centralized.

More important, the messages given off in these meetings may be quite inconsistent and contradictory. One department may be pushing schools and principals to adapt a program or activity that another department head openly disparages in staff meetings. The human resource department may be recruiting teachers with an eye toward ensuring the presence of well-educated and creative teachers, whereas the line administrator to whom principals report prefers strong disciplinarians even at the expense of creativity and intellectual skill.

The confusion that this situation creates cannot be overstated. Furthermore, it cannot be stated too strongly that any superintendent who wants to have a real impact on what goes on in schools and in classrooms—even in small school districts—must do everything possible to ensure that central office staff are "singing from the same song sheet" and that they do so even when they are in the grocery store checkout line or at a cocktail party.

I am not advocating that superintendents employ Gestapo tactics, nor am I suggesting that what is wanted or needed is a group of sycophants. Rather, I am advocating that the superintendent give high priority to leading central office staff and educating those staff members so that they understand and are personally committed to the direction in which they are being led. Among the things I have seen successful superintendents do to achieve this end are these:

- Dedicate at least one staff meeting each month to a discussion of the implications of expressed beliefs and vision for programs and activities.

- Link these discussions to assigned readings around the topics to be discussed.

- Begin each staff meeting with at least one exemplar of work by central office staff that illustrates the direction intended.

- Create an environment in which persons who disagree do not feel threatened if they express their concerns, and listen carefully to these persons. They may be right.

- Do not hesitate to cut off the head of a "snake."[8] If the snake is operating from an independent power base (newly employed superintendents are more likely to confront powerful snakes than are superintendents who have been around awhile), this task will need to be handled carefully. However, to fail to handle the situation is, in the long run, to fail utterly.

- Assign central office staff to work with principals to help develop school improvement plans, but make it clear that they are working for the principal, not the other way around.

- Involve relevant principals in evaluation conferences with the central office staff members you evaluate, and invite these same principals to do the same with those they evaluate.

Unify Central Staff

- Dedicate at least one staff meeting each month to a discussion of the implications of expressed beliefs and vision for programs and activities.

- Link these discussions to assigned readings around the topics to be discussed.

- Begin each staff meeting with at least one exemplar of work by central office staff that illustrates the direction intended.

- Create an environment in which persons who disagree do not feel threatened if they express their concerns, and listen carefully to these persons. They may be right.

- Do not hesitate to cut off the head of a "snake." If the snake is operating from an independent power base (newly employed superintendents are more likely to confront powerful snakes than are superintendents who have been around awhile), this task will need to be handled carefully. However, to fail to handle the situation is, in the long run, to fail utterly.

- Assign central office staff to work with principals to help develop school improvement plans, but make it clear that they are working for the principal, not the other way around.

- Involve relevant principals in evaluation conferences with the central office staff members you evaluate, and invite these same principals to do the same with those they evaluate.

Think and Act Strategically

Strategy involves decisions about leverage and timing. Acting strategically requires making choices from among alternatives based on an assessment of which choice will affect more of those things that must be affected if a desired result is to be produced. During World War II, strategic bombers did their work far behind the lines where battles were being fought. The assumption was that cutting off supplies at their source by, for example, bombing oil fields would incapacitate more armored vehicles than would efforts to destroy them one by one. Thus bombing oil fields was seen as a high-leverage activity. It not only hurt the oil field; it also threatened enemy tank commanders.

Timing is also important. To take the World War II example further, the Doolittle raid on Tokyo in 1942 did little directly to impair Japan's ability to conduct the war. However, that was not its intent. It was believed that what was needed at the time, and about all that could be delivered at the time, was a clear demonstration that the Japanese homeland was not immune to assault. Such a feeble effort in March 1945 would have been viewed as foolish and wasteful; yet in the context of 1942, it was seen as a powerful move and served as a rallying symbol to maintain morale while other strategies were being put in place to make it possible to strike with more effect.

Superintendents who want to lead change need to have a keen eye for leverage and timing. I have suggested here, for example, that superintendents must be close to principals if they are to have any real impact on what occurs in schools and classrooms. However, dramatic moves in this direction might have negative effects if they occur at the wrong time. For example, I saw one superintendent assign central office staff members to work with building-level teams before many of the central office staff had embraced the idea that they were working *for* the principal. The consequence was that many principals saw the assignment as one more effort to interfere in local school matters as well as an effort to offset earlier decentralization moves.

---

*Superintendents who want to lead change
need to have a keen eye for
leverage and timing.*

The reason it is important for superintendents to assume personal responsibility for the induction of new principals is that this is a high-leverage activity. In most school districts, the superintendent who attends to this matter will have direct contact with well over half the principals in the district within an eight-year period, and this contact will be at a time when they are most likely to be seeking guidance in how they should approach their job.[9]

STRATEGIC PLANNING AND CAPACITY BUILDING

As a general rule, I am much more impressed with strategic thinking than I am with strategic planning. More often than not, once the planning effort is over, many of those who developed the plan disappear from the scene. It is commonplace, for example, to involve community leaders in the development of strategic plans, yet these community leaders are seldom asked to assume responsibility for the implementation of what they have planned. Similarly, parents on planning teams are seldom part of the accountability system that should be in place to support the plan.

It is also the case that many who are employed in the district will not be involved in the planning and may be only vaguely aware that such planning is taking place, yet they will be responsible for implementing it. The result of all of this is that in too many cases, after great effort the plan is placed on a shelf and serves more as a point of conversational reference than as a guide for action.

As I have argued elsewhere (Schlechty, 2000), the reason strategic plans tend to be ineffectual in schools is that most school districts are change-inept organizations, which is to say that as most districts are now constituted, they do not have the organizational capacity to support and sustain change over time. Until these capacities are developed, no amount of strategic planning will produce the results intended.[10] Indeed, the first strategy in any strategic plan should be to ensure that the system has the capacity to implement the plan once it is developed—a strategy that is too often overlooked by those who develop strategic plans for schools and school districts. For example, until teachers come to understand that students are volunteers, it is not likely that many teachers will see the necessity of Working on the Work. Developing such understandings among the total teaching force requires considerable investment of effort with little prospect of immediate payoff in terms of improved test scores.

Similarly, there are many powerful community leaders who believe that all that needs to be done to improve schools is to go back to the "good old days." But the good old days were not always that good (see Schlechty, 1997), and to go back to them would not serve the ends the proponents of this strategy think it would serve. However, until community leaders have a deeper understanding of the issues that schools must confront, the strategies they recommend will be informed more by ignorance and passion than by facts and commitments. Thus educating the community, especially community leaders, about the conditions of education is a necessary antecedent to any meaningful move toward strategic planning.

To reorient staff members as they would need to be reoriented if Working on the Work is to move from words to practice requires tremendous capacity to design and deliver job-embedded and work-related staff development experiences, a capacity most school districts lack. To educate a community regarding the condition of education and help it come to a common understanding of the issues confronting the schools require school leaders to engage in forms of marketing and customer education that most school districts simply are not organized to deliver. The fact remains, however, that until key leaders, especially the superintendent and principals, are in agreement about the nature of the enterprise they are trying to lead and until they have persuaded those whose support they need that their view of the world makes sense, whatever strategic plan emerges in whatever planning process will be of little value.

Until these and other capacity issues are addressed, strategic planning will serve little purpose other than to symbolize that something is being done, even though nothing is being accomplished.

THE CAPACITY AUDIT

Elsewhere, I have identified ten areas where there is reason to believe that organizations need to focus attention if leaders are to be effective in bringing about change. Some of these I have already alluded to. For example, organizations that are led by persons who share a common understanding of the nature of the enterprise they are leading have more capacity to initiate change than do organizations where such consensus is lacking. Similarly, organizations where those who are going to be asked to implement a change share a common understanding of the reasons the change is needed, as well as a common understanding of the nature of the change they will be asked to make, have more capacity to implement change than do organizations where such shared understandings are lacking. Developing these understandings is one of the things that is meant by the term *capacity building,* at least as the term is used here.

To build capacity, it is first necessary to be clear on what capacities are needed and the extent to which the organization being led—in this case, a school district—has those capacities. Such a determination requires some form of audit, where the goal is to describe the existing capacity of the system and, based on this description, to develop plans to increase capacity where it is found to be lacking.

CLSR has developed a number of tools and processes to support such activity. (Readers can learn more about these by going to CLSR's Web pages: www:clsr.org.) It is not, however, intended that every superintendent will employ all the tools available or that he or she will limit what is done to that which can be provided through CLSR. Rather, the intent is to encourage superintendents to give at least as much attention to developing the capacity of the systems they lead to support change as they give to the quest for programs and projects that will lead to the improvements intended by whatever changes they determine to pursue.

Notes

1. The fact that most superintendents were at some time principals probably contributes to this condition as well. The assumption is that having been a principal, the superintendent should have a clear notion of how to work with principals. That assumption is wrong. Being a principal does not prepare one to lead them any more than having been a teacher—even a good one—prepares one to lead teachers. Leadership from positions that formally bestow superordinate status requires the leader to develop strategies and approaches that are sometimes quite different from the strategies and approaches that work when attempting to lead peers.

2. When I refer to large school systems, I have in mind school districts with more than two high schools or twenty principals K–12. Mega school districts are those with more than seventy-five principals. Small school districts have no more than two high schools and fewer than twenty principals.

3. I discuss the differences between and among these types of change in *Shaking Up the Schoolhouse* and therefore will not elaborate these points here.

4. I have written extensively on these matters in both *Inventing Better Schools*

and *Shaking Up the Schoolhouse.* Readers who are interested in this topic are invited to consult these books. I also recommend reading *The Innovator's Dilemma* (Christensen, 1997) for a brilliant analysis of the reasons so many sound innovations fail when they are installed in existing systems.

5. One of the reasons that so many model school programs and pilot programs have failed to have widespread impact is that they never really belonged to the system of which they were a part. They became special projects with advocates in the system, but the moral authority office of the superintendent is seldom invested in these ventures. The result has been that these projects seldom "go to scale" and usually fizzle after the initiating principal and core faculty leave the scene.

Change can start at the bottom, but if it is to last, it must be embraced and advocated from the top. The changes that have occurred at General Electric would not have had the impact they have had if Jack Welch, GE's CEO, had not been willing to invest the authority of his office in them. And the much-touted reforms in New York City's District 2 would not have advanced as they have if the superintendent had not invested his authority behind these reforms.

6. Among other things, without clear and personal communication from the superintendent and with the superintendent, the principal is left to wonder whether those to whom the superintendent has delegated authority are speaking with fidelity and whether the messages they give off are the ones the superintendent intends. This is particularly true when that which is being communicated is affective and moral in nature rather than simply technical and procedural.

7. Discussions of matters such as these sometimes are started as the result of an accreditation visit by a regional accrediting agency or a strategic planning process. I have found, however, that such discussions are usually superficial, and when they are not superficial, they are confined to a limited number of persons and a particular period of time. What are needed are ongoing conversations about these matters.

8. A snake is a person who passively assents in meetings and then engages in negative parking lot conversations and otherwise sabotages those things of which he or she disapproves.

9. Eight years exceeds the tenure of most superintendents. The fact is, however, that for change to be lasting, there must be continuity of direction. Keeping one person in the office long enough for him or her to make a difference is a preferred strategy. Failing that, the creation of a guiding coalition (see Kotter, 1996; Schlechty,

2000; and Chapter Three in this book) is another strategy. Indeed, I would argue that any leader who wants the changes he or she is initiating to last should make the creation and development of a guiding coalition a key planning strategy.

10. I have discussed this issue in detail in *Inventing Better Schools* and *Shaking Up the Schoolhouse*. The Center for Leadership in School Reform has several projects under way intended to address this problem in a direct fashion. Those interested in the approach being taken at CLSR should consult the CLSR Web page: www.clsr.org.

Accountability and School Reform

*It is difficult to dispute the proposition that students are likely
to exert more energy and attend more carefully to tasks
and assignments in which they are authentically engaged
than in tasks where their engagement is less profound.*

The agenda described in the preceding chapters requires considerable effort from all school leaders. It requires superintendents
who are prepared to lead school reform rather than simply endorse it.
It requires principals who are prepared to assume responsibility for
developing teachers rather than simply supervising them. It requires
teachers who are flexible and creative rather than rigid and pedantic.
It requires faith in the proposition that all students can and will learn
at high levels if they are provided schoolwork that is responsive to
their personal needs, values, and interests. Most of all, it requires discipline, persistence, and courage.

THEORY, PRACTICE, AND COMMON SENSE

As they begin to use the WOW framework in a disciplined way, many teachers will
discover that much that they are now doing conforms to what is being suggested.
For example, many teachers already use problems, projects, and exhibitions to
organize some or all of the activities in their classrooms. The WOW framework

simply reminds these teachers that the problems that students address should be framed in ways that respond to the needs and values of students. It is not enough that the problems are important to scholars in the discipline or to the teacher.

Similarly, those who advocate cooperative learning must clearly understand the importance of affiliation as a source of motivation for students. What the Working on the Work framework suggests is that affiliation may or may not be a source of motivation for a given student at a given time, and it may be more likely to motivate some groups of students than others.

The idea that standards are important to learning is certainly not lost on teachers who live in states with statewide systems of accountability. What the WOW framework suggests, however, is that for standards to motivate, they must have meaning and perceived value to those to whom they are being applied. Furthermore, those who are being asked to meet high standards must be provided the opportunity to test themselves against these standards without the threat of negative consequence if they fail on initial tries.

---

*For standards to motivate, they must
have meaning and perceived value
to those to whom they are being applied.*

The idea of authenticity is certainly not unique to the WOW structure. Indeed, *authentic assessment* has become a buzzword among educators. What the WOW framework reminds us of is that what is real to children may be very different from that which is real to adults and that it is the reality of students that determines the kind of work they will find engaging.

SO, WHAT IS NEW?

The reader might rightly ask, "What, then, does the WOW framework add to what I already know and am able to do?" The answer, I hope, is additional insight. And with this insight comes the possibility of increased control over the work designed for students. It is control that must be pursued, for without control, systematic improvement is impossible.

*Without control, systematic improvement
is impossible.*

The WOW framework provides a structure to discipline the design and analysis of the work teachers assign to students. When things go well, it provides suggestions as to why this is so, and when they do not go so well, the WOW framework can provide useful insights into what might be going wrong.

The WOW framework also provides a language that promotes disciplined discussions among teachers and between teachers and principals. These discussions, in turn, can lead to the sharing of insights and thus to overall improvement of the quality of the experiences in a school as well as in individual classrooms.

In many ways, the WOW framework is little more than common sense. This does not mean, however, that it is without a theoretical base or is oblivious to research. As Willard Waller ([1932] 1967) wrote many years ago, "In the present state of our science, [a writer cannot] hope to get very far in front of commonsense, and he is usually fortunate if he does not fall behind it" (p. 3).

In the seventy years since Waller wrote these words, educational research has done much to bolster our understanding of what goes on in schools and classrooms. Unfortunately, much that researchers have found to be so has yet to be translated into routine practice in schools. Is this because teachers are resistant to change or ignorant about the research? Perhaps this is so in some cases. More likely, however, the explanation lies elsewhere. Again, Waller's words are instructive:

> When theory is not based upon existing practice, a great hiatus appears between theory and practice, and the consequence is that the progressiveness of theory does not affect the conservatism of practice. The student teacher learns the most advanced theory of education and goes out from the school with a firm determination to put it into practice. But he finds that this theory gives him little help in dealing with the concrete situation that faces him. After a few attempts to translate theories into educational practice, he gives up and takes his guidance from conventional sources, from the advice of older teachers, the proverbs of the fraternity, and the commandments of the principals. It is this

failure of the science of education to deal with the actualities that largely accounts for the slow pace of progress in educational practice [pp. 192–193].

The WOW framework is intended to make it possible for practitioners to share their wisdom in a disciplined way and thereby learn better from each other, as well as from the research available to them. The WOW framework provides a language of social motives.[1] It proceeds from the simple question: What is it that students care about that could be built into the tasks students are assigned that would make it more likely the students would become engaged and invest great effort in the task? The primary job of the teacher is to work out answers to this question every day. What the WOW framework provides is a structure within which these answers can be developed.

SOURCES OF RESISTANCE

It is difficult to dispute the proposition that students are likely to exert more energy and attend more carefully to tasks and assignments in which they are authentically engaged than in tasks where their engagement is less profound. It is also difficult to argue with the notion that students who exert more energy and attend more carefully are likely to learn more than their less energized colleagues. It should, therefore, be relatively easy to persuade persons who are concerned about increasing learning in schools that an effort to increase the number of students who are authentically engaged in schoolwork is a worthy pursuit. Unfortunately, this is not always so, for several reasons:

- In spite of the rhetoric that insists that every child can learn at high levels, it remains the case that many Americans, including many educators, really do not believe that most students—let alone nearly all students—are capable of high levels of academic achievement. For many, high levels of academic learning are perceived to be accessible to only a few. Academic learning is an elite enterprise.

- Serious efforts to design schoolwork that is authentically engaging to most students most of the time probably cannot be done without considerably more opportunities for collegial interaction than is typical in most schools today. It also requires considerably more time than is available to the typical teacher in the typical school.

- The way the standards movement is evolving in America, many teachers perceive a contradiction between what the WOW framework calls on them to do and what they are expected to do to "raise test scores." Some teachers, in fact, frame the issue as a stark choice between improving instruction and improving test scores. Given the pressure to improve test scores, sometimes these teachers do not find the WOW framework inspiring.

Because each of these conditions constitutes a barrier to the effective implementation of the WOW framework, the final pages of this book are dedicated to discussing each in detail.

Every Child Can Learn

The idea that every child can learn at high levels has considerable ideological appeal, especially to educators who are committed to the proposition that excellence and equity are mutually supportive values. However, to say that all children can learn at high levels is not enough. Anyone who makes this statement is obliged to stipulate what is to be learned and to stipulate as well what is meant by "at high levels."

It is clear, for example, that every child will not be able to learn physics at the level this subject was understood by Albert Einstein. Is it, however, reasonable to expect that all, or nearly all, students are capable of understanding the role Einstein played in revolutionizing thinking in the world of physics?

At a more basic level, it is clear that few students will master the art of writing at the level of Ernest Hemingway or Maya Angelou. Is it, however, reasonable to expect that most students can learn to read at a level that will make it possible for them to appreciate the work of authors such as these? Moreover, is it reasonable to expect that most students will be capable of writing persuasively and with clarity? Is it reasonable to expect that nearly all students can learn to add, subtract, multiply, and divide whole numbers and work with fractions and decimals? Is it reasonable to assume that all, or nearly all, students can learn to analyze arguments critically, recognizing logical flaws, and themselves develop arguments that are logical and coherent?

School faculties must be clear about their collective answers to questions such as these, and they must be prepared to announce their conclusions loudly and to defend them. If the conclusion is that only a relatively few students can learn at high levels, they should say so. Perhaps such a faculty should place a placard over the schoolhouse door announcing, *Some students will learn here. Maybe your child will be one of them.*

If, however, a faculty sincerely believes that all children can learn at high levels, that faculty must take the time to define what is to be learned and what they mean by "at high levels." They must also be prepared to act when they find that students are not achieving these standards, and they must be prepared to be held accountable for their actions. Included in this accountability is the obligation to try to understand why students fail and, based on this understanding, to develop strategies that promise to correct the situation observed. It is only when such commitments are present that the phrase "all students can learn at high levels" is transformed from a slogan and hollow rhetoric to a guide for action in schools.

The Issues of Time and Collegiality

Although the issue of collegiality has gained more attention in the past twenty years than was the case earlier, the situation described by Lortie in 1976 and by Waller in 1932 has not changed all that much. Teachers continue to work in relative isolation and with only limited support from colleagues.

There is no question that a school that is focused on providing all children with authentically engaging experiences every day will require much different patterns of interaction between and among faculty members than is typical in schools today. No teacher, acting alone, can meet the demands that the WOW framework imposes. Collegial support and technical support from technology specialists and persons with special expertise in curriculum design and assessment will be required, and this support will need to be at a level that is quantitatively and qualitatively different from that which is now provided. For example, teachers will need to be in a position to initiate tasks for central office specialists to carry out on their behalf and expect that they will do so. To say the least, this will be something of a role reversal in many school districts.

It is, for example, unreasonable to expect a teacher to create videotape presentations routinely that support the development of concepts he or she is trying to teach. It is not, however, unreasonable to expect that the teacher might provide the framework for such tapes and then supervise curriculum specialists and technology specialists who are doing the technical work on the teacher's behalf.

If the issues of time and collegiality are to be addressed effectively, what is needed is truly radical (in the sense of "to the root") thinking about the way schools are organized and managed. It has always been the case that academic learning is best accomplished in settings where small-group instruction and tutorials are the dominant forms of instruction. Because such instruction has heretofore been too expensive to provide en masse, America's commitment to mass education required the schools to be organized for large-group instruction. For example, the idea of the school class and the graded school became prominent features in American schools only after the idea that every child should be "schooled" was fully embraced.[2]

Today, the presence of increasingly sophisticated electronic technologies makes it possible to provide all students with a form of instruction that places more emphasis on small-group instruction and tutorials than has been possible in the past. These same technologies also hold the promise of giving teachers and school administrators more control over their time and how it is used than has ever before been possible. With this control, teachers could have more time to work together, confer with students, and reflect on their practice than is generally thought possible today.

Unfortunately, schools are organized to accommodate the needs of mass education in an era where such technologies were absent. The existence of the concept of the graded school, the school class, and the Carnegie unit are all artifacts of a time when the only reasonable way to provide instruction to masses of students was through some form of "batch processing." Now, the technologies are available to make it possible to provide customized instruction effectively and efficiently. However, the structure of schools works against the effective use of this technology. The result is that the power of new technologies is seldom fully exploited in the context of schools (see Schlechty, 1997, 2000). If this problem is not addressed quickly, it is highly likely that schools (both public and private) will be bypassed in favor of new systems that have the capacity to exploit such technologies. Indeed, William Bennett, the former U.S. secretary of education, and his colleagues are already pointing the way for such an initiative.[3]

Public school educators still have an advantage over these start-up organizations. They have most of the talent in education, and they continue to have a large number of loyal customers. But if they do not respond aggressively to the need to change the systems of which they are a part, it is likely that the schools, like many of the great firms that Christensen (1997) described, will be lost.

The Standards Movement and Accountability

Teachers and principals often assert that although they would like to be able to Work on the Work, they do not have the time, and the demands of the standards movement and accountability are such that providing quality work for students is a luxury they cannot afford. They must get test scores up.

The time issue is real. Nevertheless, there are things imaginative teachers and administrators can do to alleviate the problems associated with a shortage of time (see, for example, *Prisoners of Time: Report of the National Education Commission on Time and Learning*).[4] Issues related to accountability and the standards movement are a different matter.

There is no question that the increasing reliance on standardized tests as the sine qua non for measuring the performance of teachers and schools does serve as a source of discouragement for teachers from seriously addressing issues related to ensuring that students are authentically engaged in their schoolwork. There is, in fact, some empirical evidence to support the inference that in general, teachers who encourage superficial coverage of content are more likely to produce quick results than are teachers who insist on expecting students to be involved more profoundly with the content being tested (see, for example, Meece, Blumenfield, and Hoyle, 1988).

This does not mean that students who pursue an in-depth understanding of the disciplines they are studying do not do well on tests. Of course, they do. What it does mean is that getting students engaged in ways that produce profound understandings takes more time and is more difficult than is the case if one is willing to settle for superficial coverage. Furthermore, it is much easier to conceive of strategies that produce passive compliance and ritual engagement than it is to conceive of strategies that produce authentic engagement.

Getting students engaged in ways that produce profound understandings takes more time and is more difficult than is the case if one is willing to settle for superficial coverage.

The unfortunate result is—or can be—that teachers are encouraged to give preference to programs and activities that result in ritual engagement and overlook or look past efforts to create schoolwork to produce authentic engagement. This tendency is especially likely to be present in schools that serve poor children. It is, after all, in these schools where test scores are most likely to be low and the need to improve them felt to be most urgent.

Even in schools serving children from more affluent families where test scores are relatively high, the effects of an overemphasis on test scores can be harmful. The fact that superficial coverage and ritual engagement can produce relatively high performances as measured by tests has certainly not escaped the attention of many teachers in schools serving upper-middle-class children. Teachers in these schools frequently complain that too many of their students are concerned only with their grade and their Scholastic Aptitude Test scores and are too little concerned with the quality of the work they produce or with what they are learning. An overemphasis on testing and test scores can only exacerbate this condition and may, in fact, cause teachers to become increasingly reluctant to explore more intellectually satisfying alternatives.

Policymakers and school leaders who insist on evaluating schools and those who work in them solely on the basis of test scores make the same mistake as persons who base their evaluation of corporate performance solely on profit and loss statements. Like profit and loss statements, test scores are important. But also like profit and loss statements, an overattention to short-term gains can lead to bad decisions and eventually to the destruction of the enterprise. As Rosabeth Moss Kanter (1997) has observed, "The fact that money can be counted means that financial measures can swamp other measures of performance and value and claim disproportionate time and attention—even when the counting is suspect. Sometimes financial measures are not the right ones for strategic decision making" (p. 278).

Equally important to profit and test scores is the quality of plans for addressing issues that come up when test scores or profit and loss statements indicate that there are problems. Growth and continuing improvement and the ability to respond to changing demographics and market conditions are all matters that must be taken into account when assessing the performance of organizations and the people in them. Such assessments require much more sophisticated understandings than are sometimes displayed by politicians who insist on accountability by way of bureaucratic measurement.

CONCLUSION

Until recent times, intellectual pursuits have largely been the purview of the rich, the wellborn, and the most intellectually precocious of the less affluent classes. In America, those who made their living by using their minds and the products thereof (scholars, journalists, lawyers, clergy, teachers, and intellectuals generally), while not despised, were not held in particularly high regard. What was of more value, it was held, were men (and sometimes women) with common sense, a good work ethic, and practical skills.

Today, there is a demand for men and women who can think, reason, and use their minds well. The expectation that the young will learn to pursue intellectual matters with discipline and to understand and explain as well as to act and to do is not reserved for the elite. Now, it is expected that the schools will provide an elite education for nearly every child.

Today, there is a demand for men and women
who can think, reason, and use their minds well.

To achieve this end, schools and those who work in them must approach their task very differently than was the case in the past. I hope that this book, along with the other books I have written over the past decade, will contribute to this reformulation of what schools are about and what they need to do to serve our society well.

Notes

1. Motives are of two sorts: those that have their origin in basic needs and thus exist regardless of culture and context and those that are learned and are dependent on culture and context. There is an interaction between these two sources of motivation, but it is useful to distinguish between them. The WOW framework derives its substantive basis from motives that are learned as opposed to motives that are based in more primal needs.

2. The struggle to reduce class size reflects the tacit understanding that small-group instruction is generally more effective than large-group instruction. The inability to reduce class size effectively simply illustrates that assumptions regarding

how schools should be organized, that is, around grades and classes, make it nearly impossible, economically speaking, to provide small-group instruction to large numbers of students. Tutoring is also beyond reach.

3. This problem is not unique to schools. In *The Innovator's Dilemma: When New Technologies Cause Great Firms to Fail* (1997), Christensen makes the case that one of the reasons that great firms fail is that the structures they have created to support the way they have done business in the past are often dysfunctional when applied to new and emerging technologies. Because these structures are so deeply embedded in the system and so highly valued by participants, they are difficult, and sometimes impossible, to change. The result is that new enterprises grow up that exploit the new technologies. At first, these new firms serve customers not currently served by the existing organizations (Bennett is targeting the home school market), but over time they take over the market entirely.

4. Most of the strategies employed to deal with issues of time in schools today ameliorate the problem but do not solve it. It is my belief that until the structure of schools is changed in fundamental ways and until new technologies are exploited in ways that are now uncommon in schools, it is unlikely that the problem of time can be solved.

This questionnaire is designed for use by principals. It is not something that can be—or should be—completed in a single session. It is the kind of thing a principal might work on for six or eight weeks. It is intended to heighten the principal's understanding of what he or she should be looking for if he or she is serious about Working on the Work. Used in this way, the questionnaire becomes a tool for disciplined personal reflection and analysis.

The principal might also ask teachers to complete the questionnaire as a means of checking his or her own perception. Such an assignment could also cause teachers to use the categories suggested by the WOW framework, as well as encourage them to reflect on what is going on in their school beyond their own classroom door.

Another use would be for the superintendent to assign a central office staff member to work with a principal to complete the questionnaire jointly and then use the results as a basis for discussions between the individual principal and the superintendent or as data to be used in a seminar for all the principals in the district.

Finally, the questionnaire, and more particularly the results of the analysis produced by using the questionnaire in a systematic way, can serve as a framework for developing a school improvement plan. Suppose, for example, that it is found that there is little agreement among faculty regarding what students are expected to learn or that although there is agreement among teachers, what teachers agree to is at odds with what the state requires. Clearly, some corrective action is called for. In such a case, the statement from the questionnaire that reads, "Teachers are in agreement regarding what students are to be expected to know and to be able to do," might be transformed into an action goal, and strategies might be developed intended to increase the amount of consensus among faculty regarding what students need to know and should be expected to do.

INSTRUCTION

The person completing this questionnaire should keep in mind that the intent is to get an overall view of the operation of the school that is the subject of the inquiry. Therefore, responses should reflect a generalized view of the overall operation of the school rather than a detailed description of all students or all classrooms. It is important, however, that the respondent be attentive to the data on which he or she is basing the generalized response provided. It is also important that the respondent be prepared to share these data if requested. Thus it is important that the data be publicly verifiable rather than simply a "feeling."

There are five categories of response:

a. I am confident this is so and have data to support my view.

b. I am confident this is so, but I have few data to support my view.

c. I really am not sure about this matter.

d. I am pretty certain this is not the case, but I have few data.

e. I am confident this is not the case, and I have data to support my view.

Category "a" should be used when, in the judgment of the respondent, there are publicly verifiable facts to support the judgment; that is, there are facts about which persons beyond the respondent are aware and that are not subject to significant dispute.

Category "b" should be used when the respondent is personally confident that the case is as described, although he or she would be hard put to muster facts that would convince a skeptical or disinterested party.

Category "c" should be used when the respondent is uncertain regarding the situation. This is most likely to occur when a person is new to a situation (for example, a principal who is using the questionnaire as a means of coming to know the school). It is also likely to occur when the questionnaire causes one to think about areas of school life that heretofore had not occurred to the respondent as something that should be taken into account.

Categories "d" and "e" are similar to "a" and "b" except that the judgment disputes the validity of the proposition in question.

REVEALING THE DATA

It is expected that persons who complete this questionnaire or the questionnaire presented in Appendix B will be prepared to present the data on which they base their assertions, especially when they assert that either "a" or "e" is the justifiable response. Discussions regarding these data, and the merit and worth of such data, can help to illuminate much that needs to be illuminated in the life of the school and within classrooms.

THE QUESTIONNAIRE*

In (name of the school):_____

Questionnaire completed between (dates) _____ and _____.

Questionnaire completed by:

Standard 1: Patterns of Engagement

Nearly all classes are highly engaged, and when they are not, teachers make every possible effort to redesign the pattern of activity in the classroom so that more students are authentically engaged.

   1. Most classrooms can accurately be characterized as highly engaged classrooms.

      a.___   b.___   c.___   d.___   e.___

*This questionnaire is the property of Phillip Schlechty and may not be reproduced without written permission from him.

2. Teachers intentionally plan the work they provide to students in ways that reflect attention to building in those qualities that show the most promise of increasing authentic engagement.

   a.____   b.____   c.____   d.____   e.____

3. When the pattern of student engagement differs from that which teachers want or expect, teachers analyze the work provided to discover what might account for the difficulty and take corrective action.

   a.____   b.____   c.____   d.____   e.____

4. Teachers commonly work together to analyze the characteristics of the work they are providing students and provide each other assistance and advice regarding ways of making the work more engaging to students.

   a.____   b.____   c.____   d.____   e.____

Standard 2: Student Achievement

Parents, teachers, the principal, and the board of education, as well as others who have a stake in the performance of the schools, are satisfied with the level and type of learning that are occurring.

1. There are solid data on which to base judgments regarding student achievement.

   a.____   b.____   c.____   d.____   e.____

2. Central office personnel, parents, teachers, community leaders, and state officials are confident that they have an accurate picture of the level of student achievement.

   a.____   b.____   c.____   d.____   e.____

3. In general, parents are satisfied that their children are progressing the way they believe the children should progress and are learning what they need to learn.

   a.____   b.____   c.____   d.____   e.____

4. Those who receive from this school (middle schools in the case of elementary schools, high schools in the case of middle schools, institutions of higher education and employers in the case of high schools) are satisfied that stu-

dents from the school are learning what they need to learn to succeed in the receiving environment.

a.___ b.___ c.___ d.___ e.___

5. Students who have attended the school and have moved to other schools or places of work believe that they learned what they needed to learn while in attendance here and have an overall favorable judgment of the quality of their experience in the school.

a.___ b.___ c.___ d.___ e.___

Standard 3: Content and Substance

Teachers and administrators have a clear, consistent, and shared understanding of what students are expected to know and to be able to do at various grade levels. This understanding is consistent with such official statements of expectations as state standards and standards established by local boards. Teachers and administrators also have a reasonable assessment of student interest in the topics suggested by these expectations and standards.

1. Most teachers can articulate what students under teachers' tutelage are expected to know and to be able to do.

a.___ b.___ c.___ d.___ e.___

2. Teachers are in agreement regarding what students are to be expected to know and be able to do.

a.___ b.___ c.___ d.___ e.___

3. The views teachers have about what students are to learn are generally the same as the views of the principal.

a.___ b.___ c.___ d.___ e.___

4. The ideas, propositions, and facts that are presented or made available reflect the best understandings of experts in the field of concern and are consistent with the views and lines of argument presented by scholars in the relevant disciplines.

a.___ b.___ c.___ d.___ e.___

5. Teachers have conducted a careful review of standardized tests (local and state) sponsored to determine the content students are expected to master.

    a.___   b.___   c.___   d.___   e.___

6. Teachers are generally satisfied that those things that are being tested are things that should be taught to students even if there were no testing program.

    a.___   b.___   c.___   d.___   e.___

7. Teachers provide students with a wide range of activities that call on them to work with content and processes that have been identified as worth knowing and worth mastering.

    a.___   b.___   c.___   d.___   e.___

Standard 4: Organization of Knowledge

Teachers and support personnel (for example, media specialists) generally endeavor to ensure that the media, material, books, and visuals used to present information, propositions, ideas, and concepts to students are organized in ways that are most likely to appeal to the personal interests and aesthetic sensibilities of the largest possible number of students and to ensure as well that students have the skills needed to use these materials.

1. Teachers are careful to take student interests into account when developing units of work, creating tasks, or designing assignments.

    a.___   b.___   c.___   d.___   e.___

2. Teachers are aware that some students find the content uninteresting and attempt to compensate for this fact by embedding this content in activities, tasks, and assignments that engage the students who are not interested in the subject.

    a.___   b.___   c.___   d.___   e.___

3. If student interest in the subject or content is low, teachers are especially attentive to designing high-interest activities.

    a.___   b.___   c.___   d.___   e.___

4. Curriculum materials are available that will support students' working on and with the concepts, facts, skills, understandings, and other forms of knowledge that teachers expect students to deal with, understand, and master.

    a.___   b.___   c.___   d.___   e.___

5. Teachers employ a wide range of media and presentation formats to appeal to students with different learning styles and ways of thinking.

    a.___   b.___   c.___   d.___   e.___

6. It is common practice for students to be called on to conduct experiments, read primary source materials, and read books and articles that convey powerful ideas in powerful ways.

    a.___   b.___   c.___   d.___   e.___

7. When students are assigned books to read, teachers ensure that each student has the reading skills needed to read the book assigned.

    a.___   b.___   c.___   d.___   e.___

8. When students are assigned a task that calls for the use of a computer or other form of technology, teachers ensure that students have the required skills.

    a.___   b.___   c.___   d.___   e.___

9. When discussions occur, they are always disciplined with facts and rules of logic.

    a.___   b.___   c.___   d.___   e.___

10. Teachers make serious efforts to cause students to use what they are learning to analyze problems, issues, and matters of concern to them.

    a.___   b.___   c.___   d.___   e.___

11. Almost all teachers try to encourage students to develop an interdisciplinary perspective—for example, to see how what they are learning in a history class might have relevance for what they are learning in mathematics, language arts, and other subject areas.

    a.___   b.___   c.___   d.___   e.___

Standard 5: Product Focus

The tasks students are assigned and the activities they are encouraged to undertake are clearly linked in the minds of the teacher *and* the students to performances, products, and exhibitions about which the students care and on which students place value.

1. The teacher systematically assesses students' interests to determine the kinds of products that will be of interest to the students.

   a.___   b.___   c.___   d.___   e.___

2. The work teachers assign is often linked to a product, performance, or exhibition.

   a.___   b.___   c.___   d.___   e.___

3. Students usually see a clear connection between what they are doing and what they are expected to produce.

   a.___   b.___   c.___   d.___   e.___

4. Teachers usually try to personalize products so that unique student interests are responded to while students are engaged in what is otherwise the same activity.

   a.___   b.___   c.___   d.___   e.___

5. Students generally place personal value on and take pride in the product and performance they are asked to produce.

   a.___   b.___   c.___   d.___   e.___

Standard 6: Clear and Compelling Product

When projects, performances, or exhibitions are part of the instructional design, students understand the standards by which these projects, performances, or exhibitions will be evaluated. They are committed to these standards and see the real prospect of meeting the stated standards if they work diligently at the tasks assigned and are encouraged.

1. Generally, students clearly understand the standards by which their performances, products, projects, and exhibitions are assessed and evaluated.

   a.___   b.___   c.___   d.___   e.___

2. Most students find the standards used to assess their work relevant, meaningful, and important to themselves, as opposed to seeing the standards as personally irrelevant conditions that must be met to satisfy the needs of the teacher or the system.

   a.____   b.____   c.____   d.____   e.____

3. Students are routinely encouraged to assess their own work in terms of the standards set.

   a.____   b.____   c.____   d.____   e.____

4. Teachers routinely hold assessment conferences with individual students or small groups of students where the qualities of the student products are assessed.

   a.____   b.____   c.____   d.____   e.____

5. For most teachers, student success in creating a product that meets the specified standard is the primary goal of assessment, as opposed to using assessment primarily to justify the distribution of rewards and grades.

   a.____   b.____   c.____   d.____   e.____

6. Timeliness is important to teachers, but most teachers are more interested in the quality of work products than in time schedules.

   a.____   b.____   c.____   d.____   e.____

7. Peer evaluation and public discussions of performances, exhibitions, and products are commonplace in the classroom and in the school.

   a.____   b.____   c.____   d.____   e.____

Standard 7: A Safe Environment

Students and parents feel that the school as well as each classroom is a physically and psychologically safe place: success is expected and failure is understood as a necessary part of learning, there is mutual respect between and among faculty and students, and the fear of harm or harassment from fellow students and demeaning comments from teachers is negligible.

1. As measured by such things as the number of discipline referrals, acts of violence, and threatening behavior, this school and each classroom in it are objectively safe environments.

   a.____   b.____   c.____   d.____   e.____

2. Students and teachers feel that they are safe.

   a.____   b.____   c.____   d.____   e.____

3. The faculty and the administration in this school treat each other with respect and deference. For example, conversations and discussions in the teachers' lounge and in faculty meetings are friendly and civil; they seldom reflect hostility, snide remarks, or general lack of courteous behavior.

   a.____   b.____   c.____   d.____   e.____

4. Faculty members treat students with respect.

   a.____   b.____   c.____   d.____   e.____

5. Students are respectful of each other, faculty members, and other adults in the school.

   a.____   b.____   c.____   d.____   e.____

6. When students interact, for example, in peer evaluations, the interactions are respectful, friendly, and supportive.

   a.____   b.____   c.____   d.____   e.____

7. When students fail to meet standards but are making sincere efforts, the teacher and the students accept the failure as a normal part of the learning process.

   a.____   b.____   c.____   d.____   e.____

8. It is expected that nearly all students will meet standards at some point, and when they fail to do so, teachers or other adults work directly with the students to diagnose the cause of the failure and correct the situation.

   a.____   b.____   c.____   d.____   e.____

9. Students are provided feedback on their performance on a regular basis, not just at the time that grades are given or distributed.

   a.____   b.____   c.____   d.____   e.____

10. Students have access to the resources needed (people, time, and technologies in particular) to provide optimum opportunities for success.

    a.___   b.___   c.___   d.___   e.___

11. When a student, after numerous tries, fails to meet standards, faculty members work together to find new approaches to the task.

    a.___   b.___   c.___   d.___   e.___

Standard 8: Affirmation of Performances

Persons who are significant in the lives of the student, including parents, siblings, peers, public audiences, and younger students, are positioned to observe, participate in, and benefit from student performances, as well as the products of those performances, and to affirm the significance and importance of the activity to be undertaken.

1. Students, individually and in groups, are provided opportunities to display for others what they are doing in class and in school—for example, sixth-grade students writing stories for second graders.

    a.___   b.___   c.___   d.___   e.___

2. Parents and guardians are invited into the standard-setting process for students and function as full partners in the evaluation of the students' performance in school and in the classroom.

    a.___   b.___   c.___   d.___   e.___

3. Adults other than parents, teachers, and guardians regularly view student performances and products and comment on what they see.

    a.___   b.___   c.___   d.___   e.___

4. The work students are assigned is designed in a way that clearly communicates that the effort the students expend is important not only to their learning and to themselves, but also to the functioning of other students and the needs of others whose opinions the students value.

    a.___   b.___   c.___   d.___   e.___

Standard 9: Affiliation

Students are provided opportunities to work with others (peers, parents, other adults, teachers, students from other schools or classrooms) on products, group performances, and exhibitions that they and others judge to be of significance.

1. In-classroom and out-of-classroom work often involves two or more students working together on a common product.

   a.___   b.___   c.___   d.___   e.___

2. Student tasks are often designed in such a way that cooperative action is needed to complete the work assigned successfully.

   a.___   b.___   c.___   d.___   e.___

3. Students are frequently given work to do that requires the active involvement of parents and other adult members of the community (including senior citizens).

   a.___   b.___   c.___   d.___   e.___

4. Some of the products students produce are clearly intended to be useful to others (such as other students, teachers, and community leaders).

   a.___   b.___   c.___   d.___   e.___

5. Students know enough about group processes to analyze and evaluate the operation of groups of which they are a part.

   a.___   b.___   c.___   d.___   e.___

6. The Internet and other forms of electronic communication are used to build cooperative networks among students, as well as between students and adult groups.

   a.___   b.___   c.___   d.___   e.___

Standard 10: Novelty and Variety

The range of tasks, products, and exhibitions is wide and varied, and the technologies that students are encouraged to employ are varied as well, moving from the simplest and well understood (for example, a pen and a piece of paper) to the most complex (for example, sophisticated computer applications).

1. Teachers employ a wide range of formats and varied modes of presentation.

   a.____   b.____   c.____   d.____   e.____

2. Students are provided opportunities to lead others and are also provided assistance in carrying out leadership functions if they have difficulty.

   a.____   b.____   c.____   d.____   e.____

3. The setting for instruction is varied and includes field trips, off-site internships, and opportunities to participate in educational activities sponsored by groups and organizations outside the school (for example, the local zoo, a museum, or a symphony).

   a.____   b.____   c.____   d.____   e.____

Standard 11: Choice

What students are to learn is usually not subject to negotiation, but they have considerable choice and numerous options in what they will do and how they will go about doing those things in order to learn.

1. Students are routinely provided opportunities to select modes of presentation and means of acquiring information.

   a.____   b.____   c.____   d.____   e.____

2. Students are often provided opportunities to participate in decisions regarding the processes to be employed in assessing performance and in determining the standards by which their performance will be evaluated.

   a.____   b.____   c.____   d.____   e.____

3. The technologies available to teachers and students are varied, ranging from pencils to sophisticated computer programs, presentation technologies, laptop publishing, and so on.

   a.____   b.____   c.____   d.____   e.____

4. Teachers and students generally know how to use the technologies available to them, and easy access is ensured.

   a.____   b.____   c.____   d.____   e.____

5. Students and teachers feel that they have control over their own destiny in the school and in the classroom.

   a.____   b.____   c.____   d.____   e.____

Standard 12: Authenticity

The tasks students are assigned and the work they are encouraged to undertake have meaning and significance in their lives now and are related to consequences to which they attach importance.

1. The quality of products, performances, and exhibitions has consequences for the student about which the student cares.

   a.____   b.____   c.____   d.____   e.____

2. Students feel that the tasks they are assigned are within reach if they expend effort.

   a.____   b.____   c.____   d.____   e.____

3. Tasks are designed in ways that increase student ownership for the quality of the results.

   a.____   b.____   c.____   d.____   e.____

4. Students are aware of the consequences of meeting standards and failing to meet standards, and the students understand that meeting these standards is important to their current circumstances as well as to their future prospects.

   a.____   b.____   c.____   d.____   e.____

5. The work assigned to students is designed and evaluated in such a way that the success of one student does not have a negative impact on the success of another student (for example, grading on the curve).

   a.____   b.____   c.____   d.____   e.____

6. The work students are assigned is designed in such a way that students have a positive stake in, and care about, the success of other students.

   a.____   b.____   c.____   d.____   e.____

APPENDIX B:
FRAMEWORK FOR ANALYSIS, DIALOGUE, AND ACTION—CLASSROOM VERSION

This questionnaire is intended for use by teachers. In general, the discussion of the school version of the questionnaire is applicable to the classroom version, except the classroom version provides a more finely grained analysis of what is occurring in individual classrooms. Indeed, in the long run and as faculties become comfortable with the kind of public disclosures that would be required, the results of the work associated with completing the classroom version of the questionnaire might well serve as a database to provide a greater level of confidence to responses on the school-level questionnaire. Initially, however, it is probably wise to limit the use of this questionnaire to the teacher whose classroom is the focus of the inquiry and those to whom the teacher might invite to assist in this inquiry, such as trusted colleagues. The principal certainly should not try to use this questionnaire as a device for evaluating teachers.

As with the school-level questionnaire in Appendix A, one way it might be used is for self-analysis. Using this questionnaire as a guide, a teacher might get an increasingly clear image of what is going on in his or her classroom and therefore a better understanding of what might be done when things are not going as the teacher might prefer. Such an activity might result in the teacher's having increasingly focused conversations with students, parents, and colleagues regarding the nature of his or her classroom, which could have the additional effect of expanding the impact to other areas of the school of what the teacher is doing.

Another way this questionnaire might be used is as a framework for planning and as a tool for helping in the analysis of units of "what went wrong" when student engagement turns out to be different from that which was anticipated or desired. The questionnaire could also be used as a framework for discussions between and among colleagues or between a teacher and the principal.

There are five categories of response:

a. I am confident this is so and have data to support my view.

b. I am confident this is so, but I have few data to support my view.

c. I really am not sure about this matter.

d. I am pretty certain this is not the case, but I have few data.

e. I am confident this is not the case, and I have data to support my view.

THE QUESTIONNAIRE*

Teacher's Name:_____

Questionnaire completed between (dates) _____ and _____.

Questionnaire completed by:

Standard 1: Patterns of Engagement

Nearly all classes are highly engaged, and when they are not, teachers make every possible effort to redesign the pattern of activity in the classroom so that more students are authentically engaged.

1. Authentic engagement is commonplace in my classroom, and rebellion and retreatism are rare.

   a.____   b.____   c.____   d.____   e.____

*This questionnaire is the property of Phillip Schlechty and may not be reproduced without written permission from him.

2. When planning for classes, I always think through ways that I might use the WOW Design Qualities to suggest activities I might create or adapt that will increase the likelihood of more students being authentically engaged.

   a.___   b.___   c.___   d.___   e.___

3. When the pattern of student engagement differs from that which I want or expect, I use the WOW framework to analyze the work I provided to students in order to discover what might account for the difficulty.

   a.___   b.___   c.___   d.___   e.___

4. I operate on the assumption that most of the variability in student engagement in my classroom has to do with the way the schoolwork I provide for students is designed.

   a.___   b.___   c.___   d.___   e.___

5. I regularly invite colleagues to give me suggestions regarding ways I can make the work I provide students more engaging.

   a.___   b.___   c.___   d.___   e.___

Standard 2: Student Achievement

Parents, teachers, the principal, and the board of education, as well as others who have a stake in the performance of the schools, are satisfied with the level and type of learning that are occurring.

1. Most students in my classes learn what I intend that they learn and meet the standards that are set for them.

   a.___   b.___   c.___   d.___   e.___

2. Parents are generally satisfied with the level of achievement of students in my class or classes.

   a.___   b.___   c.___   d.___   e.___

3. When students leave my class, they are well prepared to succeed in the next grade or in other endeavors where what they are assumed to learn in my class is important to them.

   a.___   b.___   c.___   d.___   e.___

4. Students I have taught believe that what they learned in my class was important to them and helped them to succeed in subsequent pursuits.

    a.____   b.____   c.____   d.____   e.____

5. Most of the students I have taught have favorable memories of their experiences in my class.

    a.____   b.____   c.____   d.____   e.____

Standard 3: Content and Substance

Teachers and administrators have a clear, consistent, and shared understanding of what students are expected to know and to be able to do at various grade levels. This understanding is consistent with such official statements of expectations as state standards and standards established by local boards. Teachers and administrators also have a reasonable assessment of student interest in the topics suggested by these expectations and standards.

1. I am very clear about what my students are expected to know and to be able to do.

    a.____   b.____   c.____   d.____   e.____

2. I have conducted a careful review of standardized tests (local and state sponsored) to determine the content students are expected to master.

    a.____   b.____   c.____   d.____   e.____

3. I am satisfied that those things that are being tested are things that should be taught to students even if there were no testing program.

    a.____   b.____   c.____   d.____   e.____

4. My view of what students need to learn is consistent with the views of my colleagues.

    a.____   b.____   c.____   d.____   e.____

5. My view of what students need to learn is consistent with the views of my principal.

    a.____   b.____   c.____   d.____   e.____

6. My view of what students need to learn is consistent with the expectations supported by the central office and the state.

   a.___   b.___   c.___   d.___   e.___

7. I feel confident of my understanding of the subjects I am expected to teach, and I am up to date with regard to those subjects.

   a.___   b.___   c.___   d.___   e.___

8. I provide students with a wide range of activities that call on them to work with content and processes that have been identified as worth knowing and worth mastering.

   a.___   b.___   c.___   d.___   e.___

Standard 4: Organization of Knowledge

Teachers and support personnel (for example, media specialists) generally endeavor to ensure that the media, material, books, and visuals used to present information, propositions, ideas, and concepts to students are organized in ways that are most likely to appeal to the personal interests and aesthetic sensibilities of the largest possible number of students and to ensure as well that students have the skills needed to use these materials.

1. I carefully assess student interests and take these interests into account when developing units of work, creating tasks, or designing assignments.

   a.___   b.___   c.___   d.___   e.___

2. I am pretty clear on which students find the subjects I teach interesting and which do not, and I try to compensate for lack of student interest in the subject by activities, tasks, and assignments that engage the students even though they are not interested in the subject.

   a.___   b.___   c.___   d.___   e.___

3. When student interest in the subject or content is low, I am especially attentive to designing high-interest activities.

   a.___   b.___   c.___   d.___   e.___

4. Curriculum materials are available that will support students' working on and with the concepts, facts, skills, understandings, and other forms of knowledge that I expect students to deal with, understand, and master.

   a.___   b.___   c.___   d.___   e.___

5. I try to employ a wide range of media and presentation formats to appeal to students with different learning styles and ways of thinking, and I receive considerable support in doing so.

   a.___   b.___   c.___   d.___   e.___

6. I routinely call on students to conduct experiments, read primary source materials, and read books and articles that convey powerful ideas in a powerful ways.

   a.___   b.___   c.___   d.___   e.___

7. I regularly assess the skills students have with regard to reading and technology use and work to ensure that they develop the skills needed to function at the level that the activities that need to occur in my class requires.

   a.___   b.___   c.___   d.___   e.___

8. I make a serious effort to cause students to use what they are learning to analyze problems, issues, and matters of concern to them.

   a.___   b.___   c.___   d.___   e.___

9. I try to encourage students to develop an interdisciplinary perspective—to see how what they are learning in a history class, for example, might have relevance for what they are learning in mathematics, language arts, and other subjects.

   a.___   b.___   c.___   d.___   e.___

Standard 5: Product Focus

The tasks students are assigned and the activities they are encouraged to undertake are clearly linked in the minds of the teacher *and* the students to performances, products, and exhibitions about which the students care and on which students place value.

1. I usually try to link what I ask students to do to a product, performance, or exhibition of value to the student.

   a.____   b.____   c.____   d.____   e.____

2. Students usually see a clear connection between what they are doing and what they are expected to produce.

   a.____   b.____   c.____   d.____   e.____

3. I try to personalize products so that the different types of student interests are responded to even when students are working on the same product or activity.

   a.____   b.____   c.____   d.____   e.____

4. Students in my class place a great deal of personal value on and take pride in the products and performances they are asked to produce.

   a.____   b.____   c.____   d.____   e.____

Standard 6: Clear and Compelling Product Standards

When projects, performances, or exhibitions are part of the instructional design, students understand the standards by which these projects, performances, or exhibitions will be evaluated. They are committed to these standards and see the real prospect of meeting the stated standards if they work diligently at the tasks assigned and are encouraged.

1. I make the standards by which performances, products, projects, and exhibitions are assessed and evaluated very clear to students.

   a.____   b.____   c.____   d.____   e.____

2. Students in my classes find the standards used to assess their work relevant, meaningful, and important to them as opposed to seeing these standards as personally irrelevant conditions that they must meet simply to satisfy me and get a good grade.

   a.____   b.____   c.____   d.____   e.____

3. I regularly encourage students to assess their own work in terms of the standards set.

   a.____   b.____   c.____   d.____   e.____

4. I often hold assessment conferences with individual students or small groups of students where the qualities of student products are assessed.

   a.___   b.___   c.___   d.___   e.___

5. I use assessment primarily as a tool to promote student success and only secondarily as a means to justify the distribution of rewards and grades.

   a.___   b.___   c.___   d.___   e.___

6. Timeliness is important to me, but I am more interested in the quality of work products than in time schedules.

   a.___   b.___   c.___   d.___   e.___

7. Peer evaluation and public discussions of performances, exhibitions, and products are commonplace in my classroom.

   a.___   b.___   c.___   d.___   e.___

Standard 7: A Safe Environment

Students and parents feel that the school as well as each classroom is a physically and psychologically safe place: success is expected and failure is understood as a necessary part of learning, there is mutual respect between and among faculty and students, and the fear of harm or harassment from fellow students and demeaning comments from teachers is negligible.

1. When students interact in my classroom, for example, in peer evaluations, the interactions are respectful, friendly, and supportive.

   a.___   b.___   c.___   d.___   e.___

2. When a student fails to meet standards but is making sincere efforts, I am very supportive of the student and encourage him or her to see such failures as a normal part of the learning process.

   a.___   b.___   c.___   d.___   e.___

3. I expect all students will meet standards at some point, and when they fail to do so, I work directly with the student to diagnose the cause of the failure and correct the situation.

   a.___   b.___   c.___   d.___   e.___

4. I provide students with feedback on their performance on a regular basis, not just at the time that grades are given or distributed.

    a.___   b.___   c.___   d.___   e.___

5. Both my students and I have access to the resources needed (people, time, and technology in particular) to provide optimum opportunities for success.

    a.___   b.___   c.___   d.___   e.___

6. When a student, after numerous tries, fails to meet standards, I am not at all reluctant to seek advice from colleagues, parents, and the student regarding things I might do or help the student do that would make success more likely.

    a.___   b.___   c.___   d.___   e.___

Standard 8: Affirmation of Performances

Persons who are significant in the lives of the student, including parents, siblings, peers, public audiences, and younger students, are positioned to observe, participate in, and benefit from student performances, as well as the products of those performances, and to affirm the significance and importance of the activity to be undertaken.

1. I regularly involve students in creating products that will be of use to other students, read by other students, or viewed by other students.

    a.___   b.___   c.___   d.___   e.___

2. I always involve parents and guardians in the standard-setting process and encourage them to function as full partners in the evaluation of the student's performance in school and in the classroom.

    a.___   b.___   c.___   d.___   e.___

3. I often display student work for other adults in the school and the community to examine and comment on.

    a.___   b.___   c.___   d.___   e.___

4. I try to design the work students do so that the student feels that what he or she is doing is of value to others as well as to himself or herself.

    a.___   b.___   c.___   d.___   e.___

Standard 9: Affiliation

Students are provided opportunities to work with others (peers, parents, other adults, teachers, students from other schools or classrooms) on products, group performances, and exhibitions that they and others judge to be of significance.

1. I try to ensure that in-classroom and out-of-classroom work involves two or more students working together on a common product.

   a.___   b.___   c.___   d.___   e.___

2. I try to ensure that student tasks are designed in such a way that cooperative action is needed to complete the work assigned successfully.

   a.___   b.___   c.___   d.___   e.___

3. I often give students work to do that requires the active involvement of parents and other adult members of the community, including senior citizens.

   a.___   b.___   c.___   d.___   e.___

4. Some of the products students produce in my class are clearly intended to be useful to others (for example, other students, teachers, community leaders).

   a.___   b.___   c.___   d.___   e.___

5. I make sure that students in my class know enough about group processes to analyze and evaluate the operation of groups of which they are a part.

   a.___   b.___   c.___   d.___   e.___

6. I design tasks for students that require the use of the Internet and other forms of electronic communication to build cooperative networks among students, as well as between students and adult groups.

   a.___   b.___   c.___   d.___   e.___

Standard 10: Novelty and Variety

The range of tasks, products, and exhibitions is wide and varied, and the technologies that students are encouraged to employ are varied as well, moving from the simplest and well understood (for example, a pen and a piece of paper) to the most complex (for example, sophisticated computer applications).

1. Students are provided a wide range and varied modes of presentation.

   a.___   b.___   c.___   d.___   e.___

2. In my class, students are provided opportunities to lead others, and they also are provided assistance in carrying out leadership functions when they have difficulty.

    a.___   b.___   c.___   d.___   e.___

3. In my class, students are encouraged to participate in educational activities and programs sponsored by groups and organizations outside the school (for example, the local zoo, a museum, a symphony, the Discovery Channel, the History Channel, the public library, a local business).

    a.___   b.___   c.___   d.___   e.___

Standard 11: Choice

What students are to learn is usually not subject to negotiation, but they have considerable choice and numerous options in what they will do and how they will go about doing those things in order to learn.

1. I encourage students to experiment with different means of presenting information and gaining access to information.

    a.___   b.___   c.___   d.___   e.___

2. In my class, students regularly participate in decisions regarding the processes to be employed in assessing performance and determining the standards by which their performance will be evaluated.

    a.___   b.___   c.___   d.___   e.___

3. Both my students and I have access to a wide range of technologies, from workbooks and textbooks to original source materials, sophisticated computer programs, presentation technologies, lap-top publishing, and so on.

    a.___   b.___   c.___   d.___   e.___

4. I feel quite confident in my skills in using computers and other forms of instructional technology.

    a.___   b.___   c.___   d.___   e.___

5. I believe that the experiences I provide students do make a difference in the level and type of engagement students will display, and I know how to work to improve the qualities of the experiences I provide to students.

    a.___   b.___   c.___   d.___   e.___

Standard 12: Authenticity

The tasks students are assigned and the work they are encouraged to undertake have meaning and significance in their lives now and are related to consequences to which they attach importance.

1. In my class, students see a link between the quality of products, performances, and exhibitions they produce and consequences that they consider to be personally important.

   a.___   b.___   c.___   d.___   e.___

2. Students believe that they can do the work I give them if they invest the effort, and most of the time they are willing to invest the effort required to do the work assigned.

   a.___   b.___   c.___   d.___   e.___

3. I try to design schoolwork in ways that increase student ownership for the quality of the results.

   a.___   b.___   c.___   d.___   e.___

4. I make consequences of meeting standards and failing to meet standards clear to students, and they understand that meeting these standards is important to their current circumstances as well as to their future prospects.

   a.___   b.___   c.___   d.___   e.___

5. The work assigned to students is designed and evaluated in such a way that the success of one student does not have a negative impact on the success of another student (for example, grading on the curve).

   a.___   b.___   c.___   d.___   e.___

6. I try to design the work I assign to students in such a way that they have a positive stake in, and care about, the success of other students.

   a.___   b.___   c.___   d.___   e.___

BIBLIOGRAPHY

Anderson, J. "Getting Better by Design." *Education Week,* June 18, 1997, pp. 34, 48.

Burkett, E. *Another Planet: A Year in the Life of a Suburban High School.* New York: Harper-Collins, 2001.

Christensen, C. *The Innovator's Dilemma: When New Technologies Cause Great Firms to Fail.* Boston: Harvard Business School Press, 1997.

Farkas, S., and others. *Trying to Stay Ahead of the Game: Superintendents and Principals Talk About School Leadership.* New York: Public Agenda Report, 2001.

Howley, C. *Out of Our Minds: Anti-Intellectualism and Talent Development in American Schooling.* New York: Teachers College Press, 1995.

Kanter, R. M. *Rosabeth Moss Kanter on the Frontiers of Management.* Boston: Harvard Business School Press, 1997.

Kelley, R. E. "In Praise of Followers." *Harvard Business Review,* 1988, 6, 142–148.

Kohn, A. "Fighting the Tests: A Practical Guide to Rescuing Our Schools." *Phi Delta Kappan,* Jan. 2001, pp. 348–357.

Kotter, J. *Leading Change.* Boston: Harvard Business School Press, 1996.

Lortie, D. *Schoolteacher: A Sociological Study.* Chicago: University of Chicago Press, 1975.

Meece, J., Blumenfield, P., and Hoyle, R. "Students' Goal Orientations and Cognitive Engagement in Classroom Activity." *Journal of Educational Psychology,* 1988, 80, 514–523.

Meier, D. *The Power of Their Ideas.* Boston: Beacon Press, 1995.

Merton, R. K. *Social Theory and Social Structure.* New York: Free Press, 1968.

National Education Commission on Time and Learning. *Prisoners of Time: Report of the National Education Commission on Time and Learning.* Washington, D.C.: National Education Commission on Time and Learning, 1994.

Pope, D. *"Doing School": How We Are Creating a Generation of Stressed Out, Materialistic, and Miseducated Students.* New Haven, Conn.: Yale University Press, 2001.

Ravitch, D. *Left Back: A Century of Failed School Reforms.* New York: Simon & Schuster, 2000.

Sarason, S. B. *Revisiting "The Culture of the School and the Problem of Change."* New York: Teachers College Press, 1996.

Schlechty, P. *Schools for the Twenty-First Century: Leadership Imperatives for Educational Reform.* San Francisco: Jossey-Bass, 1991.

Schlechty, P. *Inventing Better Schools: An Action Plan for Educational Reform.* San Francisco: Jossey-Bass, 1997.

Schlechty, P. *Shaking Up the Schoolhouse: How to Support and Sustain Educational Innovation.* San Francisco: Jossey-Bass, 2000.

Sizer, T. *Horace's Compromise: The Dilemma of the American High School.* Boston: Houghton Mifflin, 1984.

Tyack, D. B., and Cuban, L. *Tinkering Toward Utopia: A Century of Public School Reform.* Cambridge, Mass.: Harvard University Press, 1995.

Vail, K. "Nurturing the Life of the Mind." *American School Board Journal,* Jan. 2001, pp. 19–22.

Waller, W. *The Sociology of Teaching.* New York: Wiley, 1967. (Originally published 1932.)

Wheatley, M. *Lessons from the New Workplace.* Carlsbad, Calif.: CRM Film, 1998. Videocassette.

INDEX

Performances, affirmation of, 19, 21, 27–28

Persuasion, 34n.2

Pope, D., 14

Principal support network, 49–50

Principals: beliefs of, 50–53; and communication with superintendent, 73, 74; and engagement profiles, 8; evaluations of, 68, 74; and fostering awareness for engagement, 57–58; future role of, 64–65; and guiding coalition, 55–57, 65n.4; and meetings with superintendent, 68, 73; and presence at staff development, 66n.6; questionnaire for, 97–110; and relationship with superintendent, 67–68, 72–74; role during data collection, 13; and school reform, 46; and solicitation of superintendent support, 53–55; and staff development, 58–60; study groups for, 55; as teachers, 59–60; time management of, 60–64

Products, 19, 20–21, 25–26

Q

Questionnaire: for dialogue, 30–31; to foster awareness of engagement, 58; for principals, 97–110; for students, 12; for teachers, 30–31, 111–122; uses for, 97–99, 111–112

R

Rebellion: cheating as, 14n.4; in highly engaged classrooms, 5; overview of, 1–2, 3, 9; in pathological classrooms, 6; rubric for, 11

Reform, school. *See* School reform

Resistance to change, 88–93

Retreatism, 1, 3, 9, 11, 41

Ritual engagement: and extrinsic values,

5; in high-performing schools, 41; and lifelong learning, 42; in low-performing schools, 41; overview of, 1, 3; in pathological classrooms, 6; rubric for, 10–11; and test scores, 4–5, 42; in well-managed classrooms, 5–6

Rubrics, 10–11

S

Saboteurs of reform, 78

Schlechty, P., 51, 54, 70, 80, 81

School reform: capacity for, 80–81; leadership of, 52–53; negative consequences of, 65–66n.5; resistance to, 88–93; saboteurs of, 78; and strategic planning, 80–81; superintendent support for, 53–55, 71; systematic change during, 70; top down versus bottom up, 45–46

Schools: high-performing, 41; low-performing, 41; organization of, 91, 94–95n.2; purpose of, 52; superintendent's visits to, 68–69

Schoolwork, design of, 43, 44

Shared authority, 69–70, 71

Societal issues, 38

Sparks, D., 59

Staff development, 58–60, 66n.6

Standards: dialogue about, 22–30; implication of WOW framework, 86; in WOW framework, 18–21

Standards movement, 89, 92–93

Strategic goals, 18

Strategic planning, 80–81

Student achievement, 18, 20, 23

Students: beliefs about, 89–90; dialogue with, 32; efforts of, 38; interviews of, 13; questionnaire for, 12; societal issues of, 38

Study groups, 40, 55

Superintendents: beliefs of, 72, 73; and communication with principals, 73, 74; and delegated authority, 69–70; meetings with, 68, 73; and moral authority, 71; and principal evaluations, 68, 74; and relationship with principal, 67–68, 72–74; and response to saboteurs, 78; and school reform, 46; school visits by, 68–69; and shared authority, 69–70, 71; strategic planning of, 80–81; and strategic thinking, 79–80; successful, 77–78; and support for school reform, 53–55; and sustained change, 71; and systematic change, 70; as teacher, 73–74; tenure of, 83–84n.9; time management of, 74; timing of, 79–80; and unification of central staff, 76–78. *See also* Central staff

T

Teachers: academic preparation of, 39–41; and accountability, 92–93; and anonymity during measurement, 13; and beliefs about student learning, 89–90; collegiality among, 90–91; and control over content, 39, 86–87; and design of schoolwork, 43; development of, 58–59; dialogue among, 22, 30–34, 43–44, 87; and emphasis on test scores, 92–93; and engagement profiles, 8; and estimation of authentic engagement, 31; factors under control of, 38–39; in high-performing schools, 41; and implementation of theory, 87–88; and improved focus on engagement, 42; as leaders, 40, 44–45; leadership characteristics of, 40; in low-performing schools, 41; as members of guiding coalition, 57; opinions of, 32; and parent communication, 46–47; persuasion skills of, 34n.2; and presence of principal at staff development, 66n.6; principals as, 59–60; questionnaire for, 30–31, 111–122; and results of WOW framework, 85–86; and school reform, 46; and student dialogue, 32; superintendents as, 73–74; support for, 90–91; and technology, 91; of time management, 91; understanding of measurement, 34–35n.4; and view of school, 32

Technology, 91, 95n.3

Test scores: and authentic engagement, 4; as barrier to change, 89, 92–93; emphasis on, 92–93; and passive compliance, 42; and ritual engagement, 4–5, 42

Test-taking skills, 41

Time management: of principals, 60–64; of superintendents, 74; of teachers, 91

Time on task, 15n.7

Tyack, D. B., 45

V

Variety, 20, 21, 28–29

Vision, 18–21, 74, 76

W

Waller, W., 87

Welch, J., 83n.5

Well-managed classrooms, 5–6, 7

WOW framework: authenticity and, 86; and cooperative learning, 86; for dialogue, 43–44; and motivation, 43, 86, 94n.1; overview, 18–21; resistance to, 88–93; results of, 85–86